THE BINGO QUEENS OF ONEIDA

Praise for *The Bingo Queens of Oneida*

"This book is far more ambitious than its modest title suggests. The two bingo moms, Sandy and Alma, are certainly the heart of the book. But the author places those moms in much broader contexts—historical, cultural, and social. He also liberally interweaves personal stories of Oneida people. The overall effect is to make the book more of a conversation, less of a lecture. Like me, you'll be happy to have had that conversation with the author." —*Arlinda Locklear, attorney and longtime special counsel for the Oneida Nation of Wisconsin*

"Rooted in extensive research and key interviews, *The Bingo Queens of Oneida* provides a unique picture of an economic accomplishment of the Oneida Nation of Wisconsin brought about by the ingenuity, doughty work, and remarkable insight of two Oneida mothers. Hoeft admirably places their work in its cultural and historical context. This volume is an indispensable addition to our understanding of a dynamic nation." —*David R. Wrone, history professor emeritus, University of Wisconsin–Stevens Point*

THE
BINGO
QUEENS
OF ONEIDA

How Two Moms
Started Tribal Gaming
in Wisconsin

MIKE HOEFT

WISCONSIN HISTORICAL SOCIETY PRESS

Published by the Wisconsin Historical Society Press
Publishers since 1855
© 2014 by the State Historical Society of Wisconsin

For permission to reuse material from *The Bingo Queens of Oneida,*
ISBN 978-0-87020-652-8 and e-book ISBN 978-0-87020-653-5, please access
www.copyright.com or contact the Copyright Clearance Center, Inc. (CCC),
222 Rosewood Drive, Danvers, MA 01923, 978-750-8400.
CCC is a not-for-profit organization that provides licenses and
registration for a variety of users.

wisconsin history.org

Book design and typesetting by Sara DeHaan
Printed in Canada

18 17 16 15 14   1 2 3 4 5

Library of Congress Cataloging-in-Publication Data

Hoeft, Mike.
  The bingo queens of Oneida : how two moms started tribal gaming in
Wisconsin / Mike Hoeft.—First edition.
     pages cm
  ISBN 978-0-87020-652-8 (pbk.)—ISBN 978-0-87020-653-5 (ebook) 1. Oneida
women—Wisconsin—Oneida Reservation—Social conditions. 2. Oneida
women—Wisconsin—Oneida Reservation—Economic conditions. 3. Bingo—
Wisconsin—Oneida Reservation—History. 4. Gambling on Indian reservations—
Wisconsin—Oneida Reservation—History. 5. Oneida Reservation (Wis.)—
History. 6. Oneida Reservation (Wis.)—Economic conditions. 7. Oneida
Reservation (Wis.)—Social life and customs. I. Title.
  E99.O45H78 2014
  305.897'5543077561--dc23
                                   2013045084

∞ The paper used in this publication meets the minimum requirements of the
American National Standard for Information Sciences—Permanence of Paper for
Printed Library Materials, ANSI Z39.48-1992.

To my mom, Ferne Eloise Hoeft,

a journalist and educator
known for giving and receiving comfort
with equal grace

Contents

Prologue

As a uniquely American game, bingo was like the nation itself, a new strain, separate from older European cultivars, something fresh. Bingo took root in fertile American soil and spread across the country as a diversionary pastime during the Great Depression. Through the hard times of the 1930s even churches found this form of gambling to be socially acceptable and a useful fund-raiser. Similarly, a group of women started bingo in 1976 on the Oneida Indian Reservation in Wisconsin to help pay the bills at the tribe's new civic center. This is a true story about the state's first Indian bingo hall as told by some of those Oneida women. They had no inkling at the time about the ruckus bingo was about to cause.

November 1979

On any given night, a visitor entering the gym might see up to six hundred players, many of them gray-haired, packed shoulder-to-shoulder on metal folding chairs seated at tables scuffed from being set up and taken down each session. Bingo players come from cities across Wisconsin to try their luck at a game of chance more exciting than the kind played at other charities.

Indian kids and teenagers flit from table to table, selling tickets and cards from lumber company aprons tied around their waists. They started out as volunteers, then managers began to pay them a few dollars at the end of the night if the game did well. Players often tip the kids for good service, so the kids hustle to take care of them. On a good night, a kid can go home with ten dollars tucked into jeans that now smell of cigarette smoke. It's always smoky in the gym on bingo days. Exhaled cigarette smoke rises toward burlap bags and carpet remnants hung near the gym's ceiling. It was the building manager's idea to use old fabric to deaden the echoes so that players could hear the bingo caller better. Lit cigarettes perch on the rims of ashtrays and dangle from players' lips and fingers. Their eyes, meanwhile, are fixed on the twenty-five-space bingo cards spread before them.

On the last game of the evening, a progressive blackout, the caller racks one of seventy-five balls from the machine and announces "B-four!" There's a ripple of chatter as players cover B-4 with a brown pinto bean picked from a pile on each table. Someone's bound to win soon; that's the fifty-first number called, the players say to themselves. The winner gets five hundred dollars if the player's card is blacked out by the fifty-third number. The jackpot drops by fifty dollars with each number called thereafter. Bingo managers and savvy players both know the probable odds for each game of bingo. They can reasonably predict when someone will bingo, just not who. That's what makes it exciting. A blackout is nearly certain by fifty-seven with a crowd this size. The players hush for the next number to be called. Strangers cheer on a neighbor whose card is nearly covered with beans. "O-sixty-one" is called, then "G-fifty-five." Then the neighbor shouts "Bingo!" as her friends cheer and others groan.

One of the bingo ladies comes over, verifies the card, and counts out five hundred dollars in cash on the spot. It's group gambling with the emphasis on social. In this game of chance, you keep playing until someone in the group wins. That's the beauty of it. You might come in alone, but you play it with other people. The game is more exciting with a crowd. With each game lasting ten to fifteen minutes, a winner shouted "Bingo!" thirty-four times during a four-hour session at the Oneida reservation's bingo hall.

☆

Few players at the time knew that during one particular year, the bingo ladies who handed over the cash did so at the risk of being slapped in handcuffs in return. State and county officials in late 1979 and early 1980 warned of a raid at the rural tribal civic center. Sheriff's deputies were preparing to close it down and arrest the operators for violating Wisconsin's bingo control law. As tension grew between the state and the tribe, the bingo operators—most of them young moms—knew their arrest was the probable outcome. And while they could reasonably predict who would be arrested, they didn't know just when. A raid could come any day now. Players and bingo managers were, in a sense, both gambling; the outcome was riding on a little white ball. If players won, they'd go home with five hundred dollars. If the bingo moms went home to their families at the end of their shift and had a job to come back to the next session, they'd win.

Before Indian casinos sprouted across the country, a few enterprising tribes in the United States got their start in gambling by opening bingo parlors and card rooms in the 1970s and 1980s. Bingo provided these impoverished tribes a source of revenue and offered the mostly non-Indian customers a chance to win higher jackpots than allowed in state-regulated bingo games. Tribal bingo games served as the forerunner of what became known as Indian gaming.

When Oneida Bingo opened September 19, 1976, it was the first Indian bingo hall in Wisconsin. Thanks to hard work and a good location in Brown County—the state's third-largest county at the time, with 175,000 people—the Oneida were successfully running one of the first tribally run bingo operations in the nation. Bingo not only paid the light bill at the civic center but within a year helped finance badly needed tribal programs for youth, the elderly, and the hungry.

Bingo was the tribe's first moneymaker on a reservation where about half the population lived in poverty. The tribe had no tax base from which to raise revenue. Many Oneida men left the reservation to find work elsewhere. Unemployment on the reservation in 1979 was at least three times higher than in nearby Green Bay, a Great Lakes port city of 88,000 at the mouth of the Fox River. The blue-collar town was best known for paper mills, meat-packing plants, and a community-owned football team in the NFL's smallest market.

Rarely before had so many white people been seen on the reservation, let alone inside a low-income tribal housing project. Oneida's freestyle bingo was drawing lots of outsiders, even more than Rosie Schuyler's bar and dance hall across the highway. Attendance dropped at many bingo halls in Green Bay and De Pere as word spread about higher jackpots and more games at Oneida Bingo.

Constituents complained to their legislators that the tribe wasn't following state law. Wisconsin's 1973 bingo law allowed charity bingo games with jackpots capped at a hundred dollars. The Oneidas operated under a tribal bingo ordinance and did not have a state license. They paid jackpots of five hundred dollars or more.

The tribe believed state law did not apply to games on the reservation. The issue was unclear in the courts. Congress gave jurisdiction over Indian reservations in criminal and civil matters to a few states—Wisconsin among them. But recent federal court rulings indicated that states had no authority in some civil-regulated activities on Indian land. Similar conflicts were developing elsewhere between tribes and states.

The Seminole tribe in Florida sued in federal court in December 1979 to stop the Broward County sheriff from preventing the Seminoles' new bingo hall outside Fort Lauderdale, Florida, from opening. As 1979 came to a close, a turning point also was looming in Wisconsin.

Earlier that summer, a Wisconsin Bingo Control Board inspector investigated a complaint of illegal bingo games at Oneida. Wisconsin's attorney general in early 1980 told Brown County prosecutors that bingo on an Indian reservation must comply with the state bingo control law. Despite the growing tension with state authorities, the bingo ladies continued to call games and award prizes as usual, even as they were warned they might be jailed and their workplace shut.

The Oneida tribe, led by chairman Purcell Powless, a no-nonsense man who provided for his family on wages earned as a high-steel construction worker, vowed to protect bingo and keep the games running. He told bingo supervisors not to worry. "We'll get you out of jail no matter how many years it takes," Powless told the women, only half kidding.

Tribal attorney Francis Skenandore advised the Oneida executive tribal council, known as the Business Committee, of its options. "Our advice was not to shut down bingo," Francis told me. "If those women were willing to put themselves at risk of arrest, we would defend them. Purcell said don't back down."

There's little doubt that neither side relished the prospect of bingo moms being led away in handcuffs while their children watched. Brown County prosecutors were reluctant to take an enforcement action that could erupt into a political conflict, tribal attorney Jerry L. Hill said. Conflict was frequent in the late 1960s and early 1970s, a turbulent time marked by a period of takeovers and standoffs by Indian activists, from Alcatraz Island to Wounded Knee to Milwaukee and Shawano County.

Could the tribe avoid a raid?

Tribal attorneys Francis and Jerry—with help from a non-Indian lawyer who headed the newly created Wisconsin Indian Law Center in Madison—hoped to come up with a strategy to do just that.

Three decades later

Alma Webster never told me this exactly, but from her comments and actions I think it's fair to say that for Alma—and many other early bingo workers—bingo meant more than just a job and Oneida meant more than just a place to live.

The late June morning was already sunny and warm when Alma climbed up into the pickup truck at her farmhouse in the southern part of the Oneida Indian Reservation and headed north on the narrow blacktop roads. She drove past fields of soybeans and corn separated by thickets of woods not far from the Green Bay airport. The eight-by-twelve-mile rectangular Indian reservation was largely a flat checkerboard of tribally and non-tribally owned parcels. Bingo played a role in the ongoing game for control of this checkerboard. At seventy-one, Alma had short, curly hair that was mostly gray. She didn't talk much but she was to the point. She could be gruff and curt and also quick with a smile. She'd retired more than eight years ago as bingo director but still played bingo regularly. Her three kids grew up working at bingo, and one daughter still worked there.

On this day, she was driving into the center of Oneida to meet an old friend and former coworker, Sandy Ninham, now remarried as Sandy

Brehmer. The two had been an inseparable team for years when they managed Oneida Bingo. They worked so well together that they could finish each other's sentences. It's not as if they were two peas in a pod. Their personalities were quite different, but they complemented each other well. Alma was the reserved bookkeeper and Sandy the outgoing hostess. Alma knew the numbers and Sandy knew the people. They used their different skills to support each other and accomplish what neither could do alone. Over the years, they came through many struggles together. Now that both were retired and Sandy spent winters in Florida, they saw each other less often. Their reunion today was to call on an old friend who was dying.

They were heading to see Purcell Powless, who as tribal chairman over twenty-three years guided the Wisconsin Oneidas from times of poverty into their first taste of prosperity. His support was critical to bingo and many tribal health and education programs.

Powless, a World War II veteran, was eighty-four and had been retired for twenty years. Earlier in June, word spread in the community that Purcell had cancer. He had perhaps four to six weeks to live, people said. Purcell's wife, Angeline, had died in 2003. His grown children were caring for him at home. People in the community said prayers for him and his family at churches and sweat lodges.

Alma worked closely with Purcell from the time when she was tribal treasurer in the early 1970s. She presided over an empty treasury in those days. She wrote federal aid vouchers from a checkbook on her kitchen table. The job paid five dollars a month.

Alma turned onto Wisconsin Highway 54, which curves through a wooded valley along Duck Creek as it enters the unincorporated community of Oneida. Nearby on Freedom Road is the old stone church, Holy Apostles Episcopal Church, still a center of Oneida life.

Just before crossing the 1930s-era gray steel bridge over Duck Creek, Alma drove past the tribal housing development known as Site I. It's a quiet place now, but three decades ago Site I was often crowded with bingo players who filled the civic center's gymnasium four times a week. This is where it all started, Alma thought to herself as she drove past.

After crossing Duck Creek, Alma turned on West Service Road and drove up the hill past old brick storefronts and homes near an abandoned railroad line. The former Green Bay and Western rail corridor was being converted to a recreational trail of crushed limestone. Two former grocery stores, Schroeder's and Morgan's, were long gone, though the structures remained. Two taverns, a gas station/diner, and Oneida One-Stop gas station/convenience store/casino were open.

Near the old rail line, Alma turned into a driveway that led to an old white clapboard farmhouse. The homestead had been in the Powless family since the reservation was allotted to individual tribal members in the late 1800s. Purcell had been born at the homestead. He was one of the last generations who grew up hearing Oneida spoken by elders as their first language. The house sat prominently along the old rail line near the corners of Riverdale Drive and West Service Road. From their porch, Purcy and Angie used to watch residents pass by. Many of Purcy's eight grown children lived nearby.

When Alma pulled in the driveway, she saw Sandy Brehmer's van already there. Sandy was sixty-seven, wore her dark hair in a short bob, and always had a wide smile.

Like many snowbirds, Sandy and Mike Brehmer returned to Wisconsin every summer. That morning, Sandy drove into Oneida from her home near Shawano Lake, about thirty miles away. Riverdale Drive runs roughly parallel to Duck Creek along a ridge bordered by farms. Heading southwest on Riverdale, Sandy drove past Shenandoah Drive, known to old-timers as Salt Pork Avenue. Sandy grew up in a small house at the end of that drive. Her mom, Betty Doxtator, still lived there. Along an area of one-story homes, Sandy passed the tribe's Tsyunhehkwa (pronounced Joon-hey-kwa) farm along Duck Creek.

While she drove, Sandy chatted nearly nonstop, either on her cell phone or with her passenger. That was me. I'm Sandy's son-in-law. I remember when my now-wife, Patty, brought me to Sandy's house at Thanksgiving to meet her relatives for the first time. The table was set with holiday decorations. As the new white guy at dinner, I had to wear the paper Pilgrim hat. Twenty-some years later, Patty and I live with our two daughters in the northern part of the reservation. Patty and her brothers and sister grew up working bingo as volunteers in the late 1970s. I came to learn that bingo played a formative role for everyone in my wife's family.

My mother-in-law had picked me up at our house that morning to include me in the visit to Purcell. I had been interviewing Sandy and Alma and other tribal members for a book about how Oneida bingo got its start. Purcell Powless was a key to that start.

"We have to see Purcy," Sandy insisted. She called her sister, Nancy Powless, who is married to Purcell's son, Greg, and learned that Purcell was able to see visitors that morning. Then she called to check that Alma was on her way.

Two of Purcell's sons, Richard and James, were sitting on the porch when we arrived. We went in through the kitchen and saw that hot dishes and other food had been dropped off for the family. Purcell was sitting up in a recliner in the living room in front of a TV. Framed family photos, black-and-white and color, along with athletic trophies and civic awards filled two walls and a wooden hutch. A fresh breeze carried the sound of chirping birds through open windows.

"How are you doing, Chief?" Alma asked, giving him a hug.

The former high-steel worker who had helped build the Sears Tower in Chicago and Mackinac Bridge in Michigan now had thin, graying hair, and his voice was equally wispy. He remembered at once the former bingo queens. He mentioned how his late wife, Angeline, loved to play bingo.

It was too late for me to interview Purcell, but not too late to see others pay their respects. A steady stream of visitors came and went that morning: a hospice worker; Purcy's sister, Dorothy Mehojah; sister-in-law, Lois Powless; and niece, Pat Lasilla. Pat's granddaughter drew a picture in crayons and gave it to him. Most visitors asked if they could help him in any way.

Alma, Sandy, and I came back at the end of August for another visit. Purcell was again sitting in his recliner. He wore a navy blue T-shirt that said "Native American Skywalkers Ironworker" with a picture of a man walking on an I-beam. A quilt covered his lap. Medicine bottles and a plastic drinking mug with a hospital logo stood on a side table. His sons Richard, James, and Ralph were on hand nearby. We didn't stay long.

"You were the best chairman we ever had. You'll always be my chief," Alma told him as we left.

Purcell was "part of the turning point in our tribe," Sandy told me later. "It's sad to know that whole era will pass when he passes."

Purcell died November 5, 2010, and was buried in Holy Apostles church cemetery, not far from a historical burial marker of his ancestor, James Powlis, an Oneida chief who had served as a captain in the American army during the Revolutionary War.[1] The church was packed for Purcell's funeral. Latecomers filled the foyer and the steps outside the church. Attending his wake and funeral were a number of state and federal officials, military veterans, and men wearing the jackets of the local steelworkers' and ironworkers' unions.

Purcell Powless, who served as tribal chairman nearly continuously from 1967 to 1990, is often credited with leading the tribe through a time of transformation. But Purcell was reluctant to accept credit for the tribe's achievements. He said the gains resulted from a unified effort. He was always quick to give credit to others, especially the women of the tribe.

"I was lucky to be surrounded by good people," Purcell said in a 2003 video interview with author and historian L. Gordon McLester III.[2] "I blame Norbert Hill Sr. for getting me mixed up in tribal politics. In the old days, clan mothers ran things. I worked with the ladies of the tribe: Irene Moore, Amelia Cornelius, Anna John, Alma Webster, Priscilla Manders. These good people served the Oneidas well long before bingo operations, casinos."[3]

In an interview with the *Green Bay Press-Gazette*, Purcell said "a bunch of women" were responsible for many tribal ventures. "We had Amelia Cornelius, Audrey Doxtator—they were good at getting federal money," Purcell told the *Press-Gazette*. "Irene Moore—her background was education. Anna John was interested in the health of the community. Before gaming, we built the nursing home, the health center, the civic center, all through federal grants."[4]

Oneida bingo not only helped keep those operations running but provided independent funding for other priorities such as reacquiring reservation land. Much of the Oneida reservation had fallen into non-tribal ownership due to allotment policies in the late 1800s.

Unified effort didn't come easy. People disagreed about a course of action. Purcell defended the bingo operation from critics within and outside the tribe. Some Oneidas objected to having the gym used more for revenue than for recreation. Some felt gaming ran contrary to native traditions and would hurt tribal cultural values.

"Purcy always supported us," Sandy told me.

"And we supported him when he came under fire," Alma added. That support was never more important than when the conflict reached a head with state officials over Oneida bingo.

Oneida bingo grew at a time of great social change in America: the end of the Vietnam War, the push for minority civil rights, treaty rights, and the equal rights amendment for women. While other minority groups were fighting for equal opportunity and an end to segregation policies, Indians were fighting to remain separate and keep from being assimilated into mainstream America. They were fighting to keep their community— their language and their land—from being swallowed up.

Armed standoffs with Indian activists had not been uncommon in the 1970s. In 1971, the local chapter of the American Indian Movement (AIM), led by Oneida's Herb Powless—one of Purcell's brothers—seized Milwaukee's abandoned Coast Guard station. It was later turned into a school for Indian kids. The AIM takeover at Wounded Knee, South Dakota, in 1973 lasted seventy-one days and took several lives. The Menominee Warrior Society standoff at the Alexian Brothers Novitiate in Shawano County in Wisconsin lasted thirty-four days in 1975.

Other events kept Indian issues in the national spotlight as well. The actor Marlon Brando sent an Indian activist in his place to the 1973 Academy Award ceremonies to announce that Brando was refusing an Oscar for his role in *The Godfather* as a protest of Hollywood's depiction of Native Americans.

While militant Indian activists often dominated national headlines in the 1970s, these church-going women were the unsung catalysts behind bingo's rising prominence as a sovereignty issue in Oneida. The bingo moms told me they weren't thinking about sovereignty at the time. They were just trying to take care of the kids in the community.

Oneida bingo grew from a seed planted by a group of women. But they weren't operating in a vacuum. They acted in response to what was happening around them. I've heard many times that Oneida bingo started as a way to pay the light bill at the tribe's civic center. Why was there was a civic center in the first place? How did this volunteer charity grow from a weekend fund-raiser into a successful business and a foundation of Indian gaming?

That women were behind much of the Oneida Nation's resurgence didn't surprise me. I've learned that Oneida women like my wife, her mother and grandmother, and our two grown daughters have strong opinions and aren't timid about expressing them. I found it's best not to argue. They have a power to make things happen.

Just where did this family of women come from?

The Oneidas are one of the Six Nations of the Haudenosaunee (pronounced Ho-den-no-show-nee), or what Europeans called the Iroquois League or Confederacy. Much has been written about Haudenosaunee women. Traditionally, they carried great influence in tribal decision making. Power was balanced between clan mothers, chiefs, and faith keepers. Clan mothers selected the chiefs and had the power to oust them if they didn't perform. Haudenosaunee men traditionally were responsible for hunting, fishing, warring, and defending the homelands. The women were in charge of agriculture, children, and property. They did most of the farming of the traditional "Three Sisters" crops of corn, beans, and squash. They named a matron to lead the cooperative work. They called on men to clear fields and help the communal harvest with the enticement of a meal afterward. The women were so good at farming that Haudenosaunee villages usually had a surplus of food. As "keepers of the kettles," the women were in charge of the physical and spiritual sustenance of the people. They controlled the means of sustenance. They also controlled how the food surplus was used for barter or trade. In this communal work ethic, sharing was a virtue. Accumulating material possessions for oneself was a moral shortcoming. Tribal members formed ad hoc mutual aid societies to assist others in need of food or shelter. Sociologists say mutual aid societies are a form of social capital, a reciprocal trust in which people do things for others without expectation of getting anything back in return.[5]

Haudenosaunee roles have changed over the centuries, but the concept of assisting one another was still evident among Wisconsin Oneidas in the 1970s. When one Oneida widow, Prudence Doxtator, needed a new roof on her home in 1976 and had no money, Oneida community volunteers put it on for her. The men did the roofing, but it was the women who prepared the meal that brought the men to do the work.

Similarly, Oneida bingo started with moms and kids as unpaid volunteers, then grew to the point where it could hire men and women as floorworkers, car parkers, cooks, security guards, cashiers, and accountants. It was women who ran Oneida Bingo "because it's women who play bingo," Alma Webster told me. That's true. In most bingo halls, you'll see a lot of women. That in itself tends to attract men.

Oneida bingo wasn't the only reason for the tribe's resurgence. By the late 1960s and early 1970s, the Oneida tribe already was making strides in health, education, and living conditions on the reservation, thanks in part to federal policies encouraging Indian self-determination and initiatives by tribal members. Many tribal initiatives started not from leaders at the top but from tribal citizens at the grassroots level. Bingo wasn't the only way to build social capital. Churches and veterans groups have long helped rally communities and instill values of shared sacrifices for the benefit of the whole. But bingo provided something else: economic development. Bingo and casino gaming not only raised money for the tribe but put people back to work and gave them a reason to remain on or move back to the reservation on Duck Creek.

The debate that began with Oneida bingo continues today. Then, as now, people question whether Indian gaming will be a tool that strengthens tribal culture or hastens its end. At the very least, Oneida Bingo helped Oneida people bond together in a collective effort as well as bridge Oneidas into the broader non-Indian community at a critical time in history. This book focuses on the decade 1975–1985, when much of the tribe's modern infrastructure was laid.

The story of Oneida Bingo mirrored the struggles elsewhere in Indian Country in the 1970s. The Oneida Bingo conflict with state agents posed legal questions that went to the foundation of American Indian law. Why are Native Americans treated differently than other minorities? The federal government entered into treaties with Indians not because of their race, but because they are separate political groups that retained limited self-governing ability after Europeans arrived.

So first, let's back up. It's necessary to tell how the Oneidas took up arms alongside American patriots in the Revolutionary War—and against their Haudenosaunee brothers and sisters—and how they were pushed out of their homelands in upstate New York and came to resettle in a western territory that would become Wisconsin.

Notes

1. "Veterans Gather to Honor Captain Powlis," *Kalihwisaks,* November 23, 2005. While hundreds of Oneida served in the Revolutionary War, documentation of names and deeds is rare. Rarer still are graves of patriot veterans in Wisconsin. Captain Powlis is one of only forty such veterans known to be buried in the Badger State, according to the Wisconsin Society Sons of the American Revolution. Captain Powlis served from 1777 to 1784 in the Continental Army. He moved to Wisconsin with his family after his wife, Nelly, died. He died in Oneida, Wisconsin, in 1849 at age ninety-nine. His pension papers were filed by his son, Henry Powlis, in 1853. Purcell Powless was a great-great-great-grandson of James Powlis.
2. Purcell Powless, Oneida Elder Interview with L. Gordon McLester III, Oneida Cultural Heritage Department, 2003.
3. Purcell Powless, "My School Days," in *The Oneida Indians in the Age of Allotment, 1860–1920,* ed. Laurence M. Hauptman and L. Gordon McLester III (Norman: University of Oklahoma Press, 2006).
4. "Oneida: A Nation Emerges," *Green Bay Press-Gazette,* December 9, 2001.
5. Robert D. Putnam, *Bowling Alone: The Collapse and Revival of American Community* (New York: Simon & Schuster, 2000). Putnam lamented the increasing disconnection of Americans as characterized by declining participation in PTA, church, recreation clubs, political parties, and bowling leagues. Social bonding looks inward to reinforce group identities and acts as a glue to connect people. Social bridging looks outward to empower people to collaborate across diverse social cleavages.

CHAPTER 1

"B-4" Bingo

ONEIDA TRIBAL member Charles "Chaz" Wheelock has worked for the Wisconsin tribe in many capacities. Chaz has dark hair and a mischievous grin that make him seem younger than his sixty years. He managed the tribe's Iroquois Farms operation back in the 1970s. He also worked on the Oneida land claim issue and lived in the homelands area. I asked if he knew any stories about Oneida Bingo from the old days.

"Sure," he said. "B-4."

B-4 what? I was confused.

"No. Before," he said. "As in before bingo, the Haudenosaunee were always involved in trade and commerce. You should go back and look into that history." I met with Chaz for lunch at Grama's Diner in Oneida to talk about life B-4 bingo. That was a convenient spot, since you could run into most of the community there. It's at the top of the hill near the old rail line. The glass-walled diner, attached to a gas station, has booths and tables to handle the breakfast and lunch crowd. Chaz ordered a side pork sandwich and talked on a wide range of topics while I took notes. You have to consider where we came from, he told me, and how the Oneida survived the diaspora of resettlement west.

"We sided with Washington in the Revolutionary War and we still ended up as the others," he said.

Chaz talked about the boarding school era, resistance to assimilation, and renewing connections to the land. He was also concerned about the danger of gaming's success in light of past termination policies.

A common concept in Haudenosaunee culture is to make decisions for seven generations. One way of viewing seven generations, he said, is to consider actions in light of the present generation, as well as looking back three generations and ahead three generations.

"Bingo wasn't just about gaming dollars; it was about exercising our sovereignty," he said. "Those women who ran bingo were paying bills and buying basketballs for the present generation." But their actions no doubt were made with the knowledge of what had come before, and that those actions would have consequences for future generations, he said.

As tribal historian, Loretta (Ellis) Metoxen has worked to preserve Oneida heritage and memories of the past. That the Oneida survived as a community in light of what they've been through is remarkable, she said.

"It's a miracle any of us are here," Loretta told me in an interview at her office in the Oneida Cultural Heritage Department. Loretta is an outspoken woman who has overcome many hardships. She was born in 1932 to Peter Paul Kurowski and Grace (Skenandore) Kurowski. Her father lost his right hand in a wood conveyor accident while working at Hoberg's paper mill in Green Bay in 1941, just before Loretta turned nine. He nearly died of shock and remained hospitalized for a month.

The family later bought a farm in Oneida. Peter taught Loretta to drive a car at age fourteen so she could help with farm chores and care for her younger siblings. After high school, and at the start of the Korean War, Loretta joined the air force and served sixteen years. She returned to Oneida as a single parent of six kids in 1966. She married Floyd Metoxen in 1976 and gained seven stepchildren. She served on the Business Committee, the elected tribal council, from 1967 to 1996, and since then has been tribal historian. At age eighty, she'd survived bouts of cancer and showed no signs of slowing down. She'd remained in demand as a speaker and was always willing to share her knowledge of Oneida history.

Loretta said that after contact with European settlers, the Oneida and other eastern tribes were decimated by smallpox, measles, and other diseases to a fraction of their earlier population. Native nations traded beaver furs for European guns and tools. "We had to do a dance to stay friendly with all of them, but it didn't work," she said. A trade alliance with the French made you an enemy to the English, for example. The Oneida eventually were drawn into alliances and wars against the French, Dutch, English, and Americans.

"Those who survived disease and war often starved to death," she said. After the Revolutionary War, the Oneida were disheartened and in a weakened condition. Their lands were lost. The government urged them to move west. The Oneida left their animals behind and took only what tools and seed corn they could carry, she said. Along the way, they struggled with old people dying and children being born.

"How did they manage to survive?" she asked.

The traditional Haudenosaunee homelands stretch across much of what is now upstate New York, thirty or so miles from Albany and west to the Genesee River. It's a beautiful area of wooded hills and valleys and finger lakes. Today, people can drive through the area on Interstate 90, which runs roughly parallel to the Mohawk River between Albany and Utica. Before roads, people depended on waterways to get around.

The area is home to six nations that had formed an alliance called the Haudenosaunee, or People of the Longhouse. The traditional longhouse was kind of an early apartment complex of extended families. It was a long, bark-covered dwelling divided into compartments for each nuclear family. The longhouse also was a metaphor for the structure of the whole alliance. The Mohawk protected the eastern door of the longhouse, then the Oneida, the Onondaga at the center fire, the Cayuga next, and the Seneca guarding the western door. Known to Europeans as the Iroquois League or Iroquois Confederacy, the Haudenosaunee were renowned warriors who formed a peace alliance among themselves and represented a unified force against their enemies. The Tuscarora, a related Iroquoian tribe, were accepted as the sixth nation between 1711 and 1724 after they were pushed out of their homelands in the Carolinas. Welcoming outsiders into the fold was known as "extending the rafters" of the longhouse.

The Oneida called themselves *Onyota'a:ka*, or the People of the Standing Stone. According to one legend, whenever the Oneida moved their villages, a standing stone appeared and stayed with them.

The Oneida occupied the high ground, where waters flowed downhill all around them, west to Oneida Lake and Lake Ontario and east to the Mohawk River. In the heart of Oneida territory was a portage spot called the Oneida Carrying Place. It marked the only barrier in a water route through the region. The native nations had long made use of the trail route, carrying their canoes and boats across a two- to six-mile stretch of land to connect to the Mohawk River to the east and Wood Creek to the west. The carry allowed trade goods such as furs to move between the Great Lakes and the Atlantic Seaboard. The Mohawk Valley was an important east-west trade route between the Adirondack Mountains to the north and the Catskills to the south. Europeans recognized the strategic importance of the Oneida Carry and fought for control of it as well as the entire Mohawk Valley. The British, during the Seven Years' War with France, built Fort Stanwix near the carry in 1758 to protect the supply route. Rebuilt by the Americans in 1776, Fort Stanwix would play a vital role in the ensuing Revolutionary War.

Fort Stanwix, outside present-day Rome, New York, is now a national monument. The Erie Canal flows south of town through what was the Oneida Carry. Volunteer historians dressed in frontier-style clothes tell visitors how the American victory at Fort Stanwix contributed to the British defeat at Saratoga in 1777. Rising tensions in the mid-1770s drove wedges between the Six Nations and forced individual nations to choose sides. The Mohawk had long-established ties with Sir William Johnson, the British superintendent for northern Indian affairs, and many Mohawk remained loyal to the Crown. By the time of the American Revolution, most Onondaga, Cayuga, and Seneca had also sided with Britain, believing its promises and treaty commitments to the Six Nations would keep its colonial settlers from encroaching on Indian lands. Most Oneida and Tuscarora, however, sided with the colonists, in part because of the influence of a Presbyterian missionary, Samuel Kirkland, who lived among them. Kirkland, who was trained in rebellious New England, openly sympathized with the disenfranchised colonists and favored the patriot cause. The Oneida also resented Sir William Johnson's failures to respect and protect the Oneida land base. Under pressure from Johnson, the Oneida had been forced to cede a large parcel of land, including the Oneida Carrying Place, to Britain in the Treaty of Fort Stanwix in 1768.[1]

After Sir William's death in 1774, his nephew, Guy Johnson, was named his successor. Guy Johnson continued his uncle's policy of divide and rule by working to block intertribal alliances among native nations.

Among the Oneida who resented the British was a veteran warrior named Honyere (pronounced Honor-ray) Doxtator. Honyere, who served with the British in the Seven Years' War, was in his fifties at the start of the Revolution. He and his brother, Honyost, were likely born of a father of German descent (Dachstatter) and a Mohawk mother, and grew up as Oneida. Honyere, Honyost, and other Oneida warriors prepared to side with the colonists against an invading British force that was heading into Oneida territory in the summer of 1777. Honyere and his family were prosperous farmers by Oneida standards. Honyere was quite a gentleman in his demeanor and carried a sword at his side, indicating his rank as captain or war leader.[2]

British general John Burgoyne's army of regular soldiers, Canadian militia, and Indian warriors had crossed Lake Champlain from Canada and captured Fort Ticonderoga. Burgoyne planned to march to Albany and link up with Sir William Howe's command along the Hudson. A diversionary force led by Col. Barry St. Leger, aided by pro-British Haudenosaunee warriors, planned to besiege and capture Fort Stanwix, move through the Mohawk Valley, and connect with Burgoyne in Albany. Joining St. Leger's force was a group of warriors led by a young Mohawk, Joseph Brant. He was a brother of Molly Brant, the common-law widow of Sir William Johnson. Brant's men encircled Fort Stanwix until St. Leger's force could arrive. Honyere's wife slipped out of the fort, obtained a horse, and rode to Fort Dayton to warn patriots that the enemy was at hand.[3]

Nicholas Herkimer, brigadier general of the Tryon County Militia, quickly rounded up a patriot force of mostly white farmers, laborers, and Oneida warriors to help reinforce Fort Stanwix. Molly Brant heard about reinforcements coming and warned her brother that Herkimer soon would be ten or twelve miles from the fort with eight hundred rebel militia. Joseph Brant urged St. Leger to send a force in a surprise attack. On August 6, 1777, Herkimer and his force were on their way to the fort when they descended into a ravine near Oriskany. Waiting there were five hundred Loyalist troops, about four hundred of them Indians, including Seneca chiefs. The ambush caught the rebels by surprise. Herkimer, riding a large white horse, was mortally wounded by a musket shot to his leg and was carried onto a ridge.

The Oneida warrior Blatcop, armed with a tomahawk, rushed into the fray, knocking right and left. He tomahawked a pro-British Indian, breaking his own arm in the effort. Honyere, his wife, and his son all fired at the enemy. When a musket ball struck Honyere in the right wrist, his wife took over the job of loading rifles for him while he continued to shoot. After three hours, a thundershower drenched the battlefield, reducing visibility and causing an hour-long lull in the fighting. Herkimer managed to organize survivors into defensive circles. When the rain subsided, the British tried one final drive. The Loyalists turned their coats inside out and marched toward the rebels as though they were an American relief force coming from the fort. They had hoped to confuse the rebels long enough to catch them in another surprise attack. But a patriot militiaman recognized one man as a Loyalist neighbor and exposed the ruse. Hand-to-hand fighting continued with musket butts and knives. The pro-British force, weary from fighting, eventually decided to pull back.

What came to be known as the Battle of Oriskany was one of the bloodiest battles in the north during the war. The patriots lost about 450 fighters, including Herkimer, who died ten days later of his injuries. Loyalist losses were about 150, including the deaths of at least five Seneca chiefs. It's debatable which side won the fight. Both sides claimed victory. The patriots held their ground on the ridge but failed in their objective to reinforce the fort. The British eventually lifted the siege of Fort Stanwix and St. Leger's force retreated.

For the Six Nations, the Battle of Oriskany was significant because it marked the beginning of a civil war within the confederacy.[4] For the Americans, too, the Oriskany battle was very much a civil war. It was one of the few battles of the war in which most participants were from North America. Some of Herkimer's relatives, including his brother, had sided with the British. It was Loyalist neighbor against patriot neighbor, Mohawk sister against Oneida sister. After the horror of Oriskany, the Iroquois did not fight each other again en masse in the American Revolution.

Several history books cite the Lyman Draper manuscripts of the Wisconsin Historical Society regarding accounts of Indian participation at the Oriskany battle.[5] Draper's manuscript says perhaps one hundred Oneida participated at Oriskany. Their names and the number of Oneida casualties were not all recorded. Descendants of Honyere and Honyost Doxtator were among those who eventually resettled in Wisconsin.

Just off New York State Route 69 visitors can find the Oriskany Battlefield, now a state historic site. The copse of trees where the mortally wounded Herkimer was placed during the battle still stands. A stone obelisk commemorating the battle dominates the site. It was built for the centennial celebration in 1877. Until a quarter century ago, it carried no mention of the Oneida's participation.

The Oriskany battle unleashed a war of revenge among the Haudenosaunee that continued through the end of the war. Honyost distinguished himself at the siege of Fort Stanwix as a lieutenant under Gen. Peter Gansevoort.[6] Honyere was among the colonial force that later pillaged Molly Brant's home after she fled to Canada. In retaliation, her brother Joseph Brant and his Loyalist warriors attacked and burned Oneida villages. The attacks devastated the Oneida and many sought refuge in camps near Albany.

About a dozen Oneida warriors received officer commissions in the Continental Army during the Revolutionary War. An Oneida force joined Washington's Continental Army at Valley Forge in the winter of 1777–1778 and brought some of their corn crop to share. According to Oneida oral legend, the sole woman in the Oneida party, Polly Cooper, showed the soldiers how to prepare hulled corn soup, a mainstay of their diet. Oneida lore says a grateful Martha Washington gave Polly Cooper a shawl, which still remains with Cooper's descendants.[7]

In gratitude for their military assistance during the Revolutionary War, the federal government said the Oneida would be secure in possession of six million acres as settled in the Treaty of Fort Stanwix of 1784. The treaty assured the two faithful nations, the Oneida and the Tuscarora, of continued possession of their lands, but resulted in loss of land for the four hostile Haudenosaunee nations, the Mohawk, Onondaga, Cayuga, and Seneca. By rewarding the two loyal tribes and punishing the other four, the 1784 treaty drove the wedge deeper to split the confederacy.

Despite federal assurances that the Oneida would be secure in possession of their lands, New York state officials from 1785 on made illegal treaties with Haudenosaunee nations for their land. Because of the significance of the Oneida Carry, developers planned to run a canal straight through Oneida land. Oneida missionary Samuel Kirkland encouraged the sale of Oneida lands to whites.

The Treaty of Canandaigua ten years later, in November 1794, restored some of the Seneca lands. This treaty, and a second one specifically with the Oneida in December of that year, counted on the Six Nations to be allies of the United States if war erupted again. That was a real fear. The

United States had a small army and at that time was fighting the tribes of the Northwest Confederacy. It couldn't afford to have any of the Six Nations join the hostile Indians as enemies. The United States also didn't want the Six Nations to ally with Britain should war come again.

The Oneida found themselves once again as allies of the United States in the War of 1812. In 1814, a military force of mostly Oneida warriors, sprinkled with Brothertown, Onondaga, and Stockbridge Indians, played a key part in the American victory against the British at Sandy Creek. That battle was vital to the defense of the American ship-launching center of Sackets Harbor on Lake Ontario. Among the Oneida warriors was a fourteen-year-old boy, Daniel Bread, who would become a leader of the Oneida when they resettled west. Historians say it's unclear who won the War of 1812, though it soon would be clear the Native nations lost.

With the building of the Erie Canal beginning in 1817, many Oneida foresaw their days in their homelands dwindling. Federal officials began talking about removal of the Six Nations to the west. Also pushing removal were land speculators and missionaries. Rev. Eleazer Williams, a Mohawk Episcopalian catechist who began ministering to the Oneida in 1816, saw himself as a self-styled Moses leading the people west. But his actions promoted his own interests and that of the Ogden Land Company ahead of his flock's.

The young leader Daniel Bread opposed removal at first but agreed to it reluctantly as he saw the dispossessed Oneida had few alternatives. In 1820, Bread was chosen as a delegate to explore Michigan Territory and negotiate with the Menominee and Ho-Chunk tribes to buy land in the Fox River valley for a new Oneida home. He was among the Oneida leaders who traveled west in 1821 and 1822 to establish two settlements in Michigan Territory.

The journey west was incredibly hard. Most Oneida had to walk to Buffalo, New York, where they boarded sailing ships or early paddle-wheel steamboats to travel through the Great Lakes of Erie, Huron, and Michigan, then past Death's Door to enter the bay of Green Bay. A French trading post that would become the city of Green Bay was established where the Fox River emptied into the bay. The Oneida brought only the utensils and implements they could carry with them. They were on their own to build shelter and find food.

The Oneida settlements in the Fox River valley were later consolidated on an eight-by-twelve-mile stretch of land along Duck Creek, southwest of Green Bay, where the Oneida territory remains today. An army outpost, Fort Howard, was on the west bank of the Fox River.

Daniel Bread was instrumental in establishing a viable Oneida community at Duck Creek. Bread's four-decade career in Oneida politics, however, long has been overshadowed by the charismatic Eleazer Williams, who has received undue credit for his role leading the Oneida west.[8]

Bread and Reverend Williams grew apart after 1822, with Bread's influence and role expanding. Many Oneida questioned Williams's loyalties, and some were offended by his 1823 marriage to thirteen-year-old Madeleine Jourdain, who came from a prominent Franco-Menominee family. Williams was granted 4,800 acres of land and moved with his wife to a cabin along the west bank of the Fox River south of De Pere. Williams resigned from ministering to the Oneida in 1833 and spent the rest of his life moving between Wisconsin and the St. Regis reservation in Canada. Strangely, the man is remembered more for myth than reality: Williams claimed he was the Lost Dauphin of France. The dauphin, or prince, was rumored to have been smuggled out of prison in France and taken to America during the French Revolution. Most scholars today believe the dauphin was executed in prison after his parents, King Louis XVI and Queen Marie Antoinette, were beheaded, nullifying Williams's claim.

Eleazer Williams died at St. Regis in 1858. His widow lived at the hillside cabin near De Pere until her death. The Williams homesite, with a scenic view overlooking the Fox River, is now Lost Dauphin Park in the town of Lawrence, located along Lost Dauphin Road.

No sooner had the Oneida arrived in Green Bay than they found they faced the same pressures that forced them to leave New York. Now they were up against the possibility of removal to the Indian territory west of the Mississippi River. That was the proposition of President Andrew Jackson's administration, which supported the Indian Removal Act of 1830. Under the act, the president could exchange western land for eastern land held by tribes.

Jackson urged voluntary relocation but endorsed use of the military if necessary to remove tribes.

Daniel Bread led efforts among the Oneida not to budge. They were determined to stay on Duck Creek. Bread, acting as chief, made two trips to Washington, DC, in 1830 and in 1831, to lobby officials including President Jackson on behalf of keeping the Oneida in their new home in Michigan Territory. Bread lobbied intensely for four months in Washington. He was in the capitol at the same time the Cherokee Nation was suing the state of Georgia before the US Supreme Court. The Cherokee were trying to gain federal treaty rights to remain in their homelands in the Southeast. Washington City, as it was called then, was abuzz with talk about what the court under Chief Justice John Marshall would decide, according to theologian and journalist Calvin Colton, who accompanied the Oneida Indians on their visit. Numerous Indians from other tribes had gathered in the city because Jackson's administration had brought the "Indian question" to the fore.[9]

In the 1831 case *Cherokee Nation v. Georgia*, the US Supreme Court ruled that tribes had no standing to sue states in federal courts. This was the second leg of what became known as the Marshall trilogy of American Indian law. The first Marshall case, *Johnson v. McIntosh*, was decided in 1823 and held that full legal title to tribal lands could not be entrusted to tribes and instead must be managed through the federal government's benevolent guardianship. Soon after the *Cherokee* case, the Marshall court in 1832 decided the third case, *Worcester v. Georgia*, which said federal treaties with Indian nations could not be overturned by state laws. (*Worcester* would be cited by a federal judge hearing the Oneida Bingo case nearly 150 years later.)

President Andrew Jackson's administration, however, ignored the Supreme Court ruling in *Worcester* and worked to move Indians to lands west. The removal policy culminated in the Trail of Tears, the forced relocation of thousands of Indians. Yet, because of the leadership of Chief Bread and his councilors, the Oneida in Wisconsin successfully resisted removal farther west.

From 1838 to 1846, the Oneida split into three communities: a small group remaining in New York, now called the Oneida Indian Nation; a group settling in Canada near London, Ontario, known as the Oneida Nation of the Thames; and a larger group settling at Duck Creek, later known as the Oneida Nation of Wisconsin. The Oneida reservation in Wisconsin along Duck Creek was formally established in the Treaty of Buffalo Creek of 1838, some ten years before Wisconsin became a state. The 65,400-acre reservation was based on 100 acres for each of the Oneida's 654-member population at the time.

Despite efforts to assimilate them into white culture, the Oneida managed to maintain a separate identity. They took up western farming methods and lived on subsistence crops. Most continued to speak Oneida as a first language. Daniel Bread was instrumental in adapting the traditional condolence ritual to the Oneida's new home in Wisconsin. This was accomplished through the annual celebration of Independence Day. Every July 4, Oneida chiefs made formal addresses to their people and invited guests in a conscious diplomatic attempt to soothe Oneida–white relations within the Brown County region and to build bridges with key members of the surrounding white community. By recalling the past, these Oneida leaders reminded their own people as well as outsiders of the need for ties to bind them. Though the Revolutionary War alliance cost the Oneida dearly, they were proud of their role as warriors of General Washington.[10] To this day, the Oneida powwow is always held in conjunction with the Fourth of July and begins with an honor ceremony recognizing Oneida warriors and their sacrifices for American independence.

The latter half of the nineteenth century proved punishing to the Wisconsin Oneida. During the Civil War, the Oneida lost 4 to 5 percent of their 1,100-member population through casualties or disease. Between 111 and 142 men from the reservation volunteered to fight for the Union and between 46 and 65 died during the war. A smallpox epidemic ravaged the reservation during 1864–1865 and killed 15 residents. Patriotism was a factor in enlistment, but the bounty system may have been a bigger motivating factor. Recruits could receive three hundred dollars for a three-year enlistment.[11]

In 1879, the federal government outlined goals to help Indians become self-supporting farmers. Individuals would get title to their own farms, thus fostering pride in ownership rather than tribal dependence on land held in common. The Dawes General Allotment Act of 1887 authorized subdivision of Indian reservations and allotment of lands to tribal members. It

was applied to the Oneida reservation in Wisconsin in 1891. As an inducement to get Oneida people to accept allotment, the government built the
Oneida Boarding School to educate youth. The campus, on a ridge west of
Duck Creek, contained a farm and a hospital. After nearly thirty years in
service, the Oneida school closed in 1919 to the dismay of many Oneida,
and the land fell into non-Indian hands. The Green Bay Catholic Diocese
bought the site for use as a seminary in 1924, and it remained as such for
nearly sixty years, known as the Sacred Heart Center.

Under allotment, individual Oneida were to receive fee simple title after
a twenty-five-year test period. In 1906, the Burke Act allowed "competent"
Indians to immediately receive individual title to their lands, thus modi-
fying the Dawes Act. The reservation was configured into a new Brown
County town of Hobart and an Outagamie County town of Oneida. But
individual Oneida, responsible for paying taxes on fee lands, often fell
into delinquency because of poverty and inability to pay taxes. As a result, the Oneida lost much of the land. Non-Indians bought up Oneida parcels within the reservation. By 1933, Wisconsin Oneida possessed less than
ninety acres of tribal lands held in common and about seven hundred acres
of land held by individual allottees.

One positive legacy of this era was the development of lacemaking traditions by Oneida women. In the 1890s, Oneida women learned the art of
lacemaking to supplement family income. Sybil Carter, an Episcopal missionary, started this cottage industry. Lacemaking reinforced what Victori-
ans understood as women's culture: the knowledge and skills transmitted
from one generation of women to another. The effort helped bind families
together while providing an alternative to the factory system of wage labor.
Their pieces sold for several hundred dollars each in New York City. Jose-
phine (Hill) Webster of Oneida ran the lacemaking operation in Oneida,
involving up to 150 women.

The federal government changed its Indian policy in the 1930s by boost-
ing funding for Indian health, education, and economic development. Congress also passed the Indian Reorganization Act of 1934, which halted further allotments and allowed tribes to adopt constitutions and regain lands.
The act was pushed by social reformer John Collier, commissioner for the
Bureau of Indian Affairs under President Franklin D. Roosevelt.

The New Deal era brought hope to the struggling Oneida. Besides construction of homes, about two dozen Oneida participated in the Oneida

Language and Folklore Project, financed by the Works Progress Administration between 1938 and 1942. Participants wrote their own accounts in spiral notebooks and collected interviews of other elders. The WPA project described many poignant and sad stories told by Oneida elders. The material is now used in teaching Oneida history in tribal schools.

The 1930s was a decade of revolutionary change for the Oneida. Oscar Archiquette and Morris Wheelock were among the Oneida leaders who saw the political and economic advantages of tribal incorporation under the Indian Reorganization Act. The Oneida established a four-member elected tribal council called the Business Committee. Although many actions still had to be approved by the Bureau of Indian Affairs, the tribal government was able to obtain grants to repurchase former tribal lands and build housing. The WPA and the Civilian Conservation Corps provided relief employment.

During World War II, Oneida men increasingly left the reservation to serve in the military or find work at military plants. Many moved to Detroit. In the postwar era, Congress pushed new policies to "emancipate" Indians from reservations. This policy, called termination, sought to end federal trust obligations toward Indian tribes and forcibly assimilate Indians into the mainstream. Relocation and urbanization policies encouraged Indians to leave reservation poverty and find jobs in big cities. Poor economic conditions led more than half of the enrolled 3,500 Oneida tribal members to migrate from the Green Bay area to other cities to find work. In many cases, the policies served to separate Indians from their kinship networks, leaving them isolated in unfamiliar cities.

In the 1950s, some states felt they were unable to address crime and lawlessness on Indian reservations, in part because federal law precluded state action on reservations. In response, Congress gave a handful of states, including Wisconsin, criminal and civil jurisdiction over its Indian populations under Public Law 280. Many Indian-rights advocates saw P.L. 280 as an encroachment on tribal sovereignty and a barrier to self-determination.

The Oneida Tribe of Wisconsin came close to being fully terminated as a sovereign nation in the 1950s. In September 1952 the BIA concluded that the Oneida tribe was ready for complete termination, meaning the BIA would end its trusteeship responsibilities. A month later, the BIA began to "sell" its withdrawal program to the Oneida. Throughout 1953, the BIA offered the Oneida a lump sum of sixty thousand dollars to end the sovereign-to-sovereign relationship as stated in the Canandaigua Treaty of 1794. Oneida poverty in the 1950s no doubt led the state's congressional delegation to think twice about carrying out termination, however, for fear the state would assume an increased financial burden.[12]

The Oneida's neighbor, the Menominee tribe, was terminated in 1954. That plan, fully implemented in 1961, turned the reservation into Menominee County under state jurisdiction. It became the state's newest and poorest county, Menominee leader Ada Deer said later. The tribe's vast timber resources were held and managed by Menominee Enterprises, Inc. Many Menominee feared that without federal protection, their lands would pass into the hands of non-Indians. In 1970, Ada Deer helped form a grassroots group, the Determination of Rights and Unity for Menominee Shareholders (DRUMS), to restore tribal status. That finally occurred in 1973.

"Mainly I want to show people who say nothing can be done in this society that it just isn't so. You don't have to collapse just because there's federal law in your way. Change it!" Ada told a *Washington Post* reporter.

Ada Deer served as Menominee tribal chair from 1974 to 1976 and headed the Menominee Restoration Committee. She headed the US Bureau of Indian Affairs from 1993 to 1997, the first woman to do so, and now is a lecturer and director of the American Indian Studies Department at UW–Madison.

I asked her what made native women strong.

"It's not magical," she told me. "It's just that women are more sensitive to the needs of the community. It's about care and concern for your people. Women's issues are all our issues."

According to Ada, that applies not just to native women but to women everywhere. Ada said her mother, who was white, was the most influential person in her life. Born in 1904, Constance Wood came from a well-off family in Philadelphia. She was fascinated by Indian culture and didn't fit the mind-set at the time of promoting assimilation of Indians, Ada told me. Constance and her sister became nurses. Constance worked in Appalachia and Rosebud, South Dakota, then moved to Keshena, Wisconsin, to work at the Menominee hospital.

"That's where she met my dad," Ada said. Ada was born in 1935, the oldest of five children. The family lived in a log cabin along the Wolf River north of Keshena.

"We were poor like everyone else," she said, though she never felt poor in spirit. "My mother had a deep reverence for people and cultural values. She told me early on that I was Indian and that I was put on this Earth by the Creator to help my people," Ada said. "My mother inspired and nurtured me. She set me on my lifelong path." Constance Deer died in 1984.

Ada Deer told me the Oneida and Menominee people have always had friendly relations, although she noted that the Menominee reservation would have been larger if a section hadn't been sold to the Oneida to create their reservation.

"We were practicing Native American hospitality," she said.

The Oneida, meanwhile, continued to hang on to their reservation during the termination era. The Oneida reservation's proximity to Green Bay afforded jobs and educational opportunities to the Oneida and a source of cheap labor to area businesses. Oneida men often left the reservation to find work in factories, railroads, cargo ports, or lumber camps. Oneida women often took buses into Green Bay and De Pere to work as housekeepers. But life was still quite difficult. They faced racial prejudice. They were often the last hired and first fired. Some homes were little more than tarpaper shacks without indoor plumbing. Others were modest but well crafted, many of them built of solid logs hewn by hand and held together by the toil of friends and family. Nearly every family was touched in some way by poverty.

Things were starting to change by the late 1960s, with the civil rights movement and Great Society programs. By 1976, the nation's bicentennial anniversary of independence, the Oneida had managed to survive in their new home in Wisconsin. Purcell Powless was known to say that the Oneida Nation had two things going for it: its location and its people. The Oneida reservation was enviably close to Green Bay markets, jobs, and schools. The Oneida people were resourceful. They adapted to new environments.

But being close to Green Bay could be a curse as well. By 1976, huge chunks of former Oneida reservation land had been annexed into Green Bay and its spreading suburbs. Packerland Drive, Northeast Wisconsin Technical College, and Brown County's Austin Straubel Airport all were within the original 1838 reservation boundaries. The Oneida had become a minority on their own reservation.[13] As the suburbs expanded west, housing subdivisions sprang up as bedroom communities for Green Bay commuters. Developers in those days were known to cut down a grove of cedars, replace it with streets and homes and lawns, and then call the subdivision Cedar Grove. In northern Hobart, developers built a new subdivision called Indian Trails in the 1970s, offering nice split-level homes in a hilly, wooded area northwest of Duck Creek. Streets were named for Indian nations: Navajo, Seminole, Choctaw, Arapahoe, Kiowa, Hopi, Fox, Wyandot, and Cherokee.

Inside the kitchens decorated in burnt orange, avocado, and harvest gold, neighbors gathered over cups of coffee. Few likely knew they lived on an Indian reservation. Back then, there were no Indians in Indian Trails. Some people might not have been aware Indians still lived in Brown and Outagamie Counties. Of those who were aware, some enjoyed good relations with their Oneida neighbors; others thought Indians were a problem that needed to go away. Unfortunately, racist attitudes continued to linger. Many people driving through the rural Oneida landscape on Highway 54 west of Green Bay probably saw little reason to stop until they reached Seymour.

But by late 1976, the non-Indian population would discover a good reason to stop at Oneida. A form of gambling with cash prizes unheard of elsewhere in Wisconsin would be drawing hundreds of vehicles into a poor reservation housing complex along Duck Creek. Another revolutionary change was on the horizon for Indian country that would have a tremendous impact on Oneida and other native nations as well.

Bingo would put Oneida on the map.

Notes

1. Joseph T. Glatthaar and James Kirby Martin, *Forgotten Allies: The Oneida Indians and the American Revolution* (New York: Hill and Wang, 2006).

2. Lyman C. Draper manuscripts, vol. 11 U, Notes on the Oneidas, Wisconsin Historical Society, Madison.

3. Some historical accounts give the wife's name as Sarah Montour, also known as Tyonajanegen (Two Kettles Together). She and Honyere had three children, Jacob, Cornelius, and Dorothea. Other accounts name Dolly Cobus as the wife who fought bravely at Oriskany. Honyere was

also married to Dolly and they had a son, Peter, according to genealogical records at the Oneida Cultural Heritage Department. Most accounts say the son who fought at Oriskany was Cornelius Doxtator.

4. Barbara Graymont, *The Iroquois in the American Revolution* (Syracuse, NY: Syracuse University Press, 1972).

5. Lyman C. Draper, born in 1815 in Lockport, New York, became fascinated by early American history after hearing stories of his father's captivity by the British in the War of 1812. His interviews with pioneers and Indians and their descendants became the foundation for the collections of the Wisconsin Historical Society, of which he was the first secretary and librarian. He died in Madison in 1891.

6. L. Gordon McLester III and Laurence M. Hauptman, eds., Introduction, "Wisconsin Oneidas Polish the Chain of Alliance," in *A Nation within a Nation* (Madison: Wisconsin Historical Society Press, 2010).

7. Glatthaar and Martin, *Forgotten Allies*.

8. Laurence M. Hauptman and L. Gordon McLester III, *Chief Daniel Bread and the Oneida Nation of Indians of Wisconsin* (Norman: University of Oklahoma Press, 2002).

9. Ibid.

10. Ibid.

11. Laurence M. Hauptman, *The Iroquois in the Civil War: From Battlefield to Reservation* (Syracuse, NY: Syracuse University Press, 1998).

12. Laurence M. Hauptman, *The Iroquois Struggle for Survival: World War II to Red Power* (Syracuse, NY: Syracuse University Press, 1986).

13. Of the 5,223 people living on the reservation between 1970 and 1972, for example, only 1,980 of them were Oneida, according to community data compiled by the tribe. By 1979 there were 3,244 Oneida living on the reservation. Non-Oneida people continue to outnumber Oneida on the reservation.

CHAPTER 2

Irene Moore: A Keeper of the Kettles

I think there's enough Indians thinking right and
thinking for their own people that things will turn out,
the way I see it. —Irene Moore, July 5, 1976

ALMA WEBSTER and Sandra Ninham are among many Oneida women who credit longtime community leader Irene Moore with getting them involved in Oneida community affairs. Until she was ten years old Irene Moore spoke only the Oneida language. As an elder, she worked tirelessly to improve education and housing on the reservation. Irene recognized skills in others and wanted them developed. She was known for recruiting people to serve their community. And she was persistent. She persuaded Caroline Skenandore and her daughters to cook for church dinners and encouraged her niece, Althea Schuyler, to run for tribal office. Irene had become involved in tribal affairs herself in the 1940s, serving on several committees, including the Business Committee. In 1963, Irene became the first woman elected chair of a Wisconsin Indian tribe. She was serving as tribal vice chair in 1970 when she approached Alma Webster about an opportunity.

"Irene Moore asked if I would finish out the term of tribal treasurer when a vacancy opened," said Alma, who had been treasurer of the Oneida Methodist Church. Irene had served as treasurer for the same church earlier. On March 2, 1970, Alma was appointed to fill the vacant tribal treasurer's position and then won subsequent elections to the post, serving through March 1977.

The treasurer, secretary, chair, and vice chair—members of the Business Committee—had offices in the tribal administration building at Chicago Corners, the intersection of Fish Creek Road and Outagamie County Road H, on the southwest side of the reservation.

Sandy was twenty-seven and a mother when in 1970 Irene encouraged her to apply for a coordinator position with the Community Action Program (CAP), which Irene had once headed. It was Sandy's first full-time paying job. The program's offices also were in the tribal building at Chicago Corners. The CAP, begun under the Economic Opportunity Act of 1964, was designed to address the causes of poverty through community organizing and federal aid.

Sandy had been working as a nonpaid home school coordinator for Indian students in local public schools under the Johnson-O'Malley Act and knew Irene from serving on the tribe's education committee.

"If not for Irene, I wouldn't have applied," Sandy recalled. Irene was about sixty-seven at the time. "She made me fill out the forms, then tracked me down at my mom's house to tell me I got the job. And then she said we were going to Shell Lake the next day and that I would be driving her car."

Irene was born October 17, 1903, the oldest child of Jamison and Ida (Skenandore) Metoxen. Her parents were born in Oneida, and their parents had been among the Oneida who emigrated from New York. Since about 1880, young Oneida were sent to Indian boarding schools across the country in an effort to assimilate them into mainstream culture. Jamison Metoxen attended the Hampton, Virginia, Indian School. His future wife, Ida Skenandore, had gone to the Tomah, Wisconsin, Indian School but because of poor eyesight was sent home after the second or third grade.

Jamison farmed an allotment about three miles south of the Oneida Methodist Church. He cut trees, sold the timber, and cleared the land. Together the couple grew feed corn and hay for their eight to ten cows. Irene had to haul firewood for the house. Irene's mother always had a nice garden of Indian corn. She also made and sold beautiful ash baskets.

"I'm very sorry I didn't learn that art. People always wanted her baskets," Irene said in a 1976 interview with her niece, Madelyn Genskow.

Irene grew up speaking only Oneida. At age ten, she entered the Oneida Boarding School not knowing a word of English.

"I did get into trouble for it. I'd be saying 'yes' when I ought to have said 'no,' and 'no' when I ought to have said 'yes,'" she told her niece. Irene was punished with a spank on the hand.

"If you were caught speaking our language you were punished. In a way, it was cruel. But that was their way of helping me," she said. "I was sent there to learn. I took it in stride."

She stayed three years at Oneida, then was sent to Carlisle Indian Industrial School in Pennsylvania. Carlisle, founded in 1879 by army captain Richard Henry Pratt, was the first off-reservation boarding school and became the model for Indian boarding schools nationwide.

"I thought it was beautiful, with very nice grounds and the grass was cut. It was like a college. But I was kind of lonesome when I thought how far I was from home," Irene said.

She learned to love reading. She was assigned chores like helping in the laundry or dining hall. On Sundays, a group of women walked downtown with a school officer to attend Methodist church services. Irene was disappointed to leave Carlisle after only a year. The school closed in 1918, and the army used it as a military hospital for soldiers injured in World War I.

Irene was sent to the Flandreau, South Dakota, Indian School, which, compared to Carlisle, "seemed to have been settled in the wilderness," she said. After graduating high school at Flandreau, she returned to Wisconsin at age eighteen and lived with her parents in Kaukauna. Their farm by then had been sold to non-Indians. She wanted to take a course in stenography, but the family was too poor. Instead she applied for a job in the same Kaukauna paper mill where her father was working. Then she clerked at a department store in Appleton.

She had met a young man, Simon "Sim" Moore, at a picnic in Oneida when she returned from Flandreau. They met again at a dance and started going out. During winters, Sim worked in northern Wisconsin logging camps cutting timber. The pair dated for three years and married at the Oneida Methodist parsonage. It was a small wedding, with just a few relatives and friends. The bride wore a navy blue dress and corsage. They lived with Irene's parents in Kaukauna before moving into a rented house in Oneida. After that, Sim worked at a gravel pit crushing stones that were used on roads. The couple eventually ran their own dairy farm near Seymour and had three daughters. In their adult years, the three daughters married and took the names of Margaret Danforth, Lois Powless, and Lillian King.

During the Depression, the federal government started the Indian Reorganization Act.

"I was interested and attended a lot of meetings," Irene told her niece. Oneida tribal lands had dwindled to about four hundred acres. Under reorganization, the tribe acquired two thousand acres, she said. Irene wanted to see land used for better housing, as some homes did not have their own wells or indoor plumbing.

She also became active in the Oneida Methodist Church as a volunteer and as church treasurer. "But I knew you also had to go outside your church, because there were a lot of things that needed to be done," she told a *Press-Gazette* reporter in 1975. She helped organize the Oneida Community Area 4-H Club and Oneida Athletic Association when her children were young. As a child, she had been taught in schools that Native Americans were uncivilized. As an adult, she wanted to dispel that negative image and worked to improve the curriculum in Seymour schools.

She became involved in tribal affairs in 1949. At that time, there were few federal programs to help Indians. "We didn't get paid. We had to do as much as we could without money," she told the *Press-Gazette*. She served as vice chair of the tribe's Business Committee in 1952, again from 1956 to 1963, and a third time from 1968 to 1974. She was a member of the council that fought efforts by the Bureau of Indian Affairs to disestablish the Oneida reservation in the 1950s.

Oneida tribal leaders at that time held their monthly meetings in an old wood-frame building at a former Civilian Conservation Corps camp, now part of the Site II residential complex on Ranch Road in the southwest part of the reservation. The building had no running water or indoor bathroom, and the men would arrive early to stoke the fire before tribal council meetings. Former tribal secretary Amelia Cornelius remembered that in winter, everyone huddled close to the stove when meetings began. By the end of the meeting, people had spread their chairs out in a wider circle as the fire got hotter.

In 1963, Irene Moore served a one-year term as tribal chair. She had been nominated for chair before but always felt the chief should be a man, she told her niece. The previous chair, Julius Danforth, asked her to run in 1963 because his wife was sick and he wasn't able to attend meetings.

"I was working on improving tribal housing and I agreed to run for tribal chair because we were already in the middle of our housing project proposal and we felt that it would take too long to introduce a new person to what we were doing," she said.[1]

She won 133 votes to Norbert Hill Sr.'s 110. A Milwaukee newspaper interviewed her and published her photo. The 1963 story referred to her as a "dairy farmer's wife," defining her by her husband's occupation.

Madelyn Genskow told me Irene's success was due in part to the support of her husband, Sim. "He allowed Irene to be a leader," Madelyn said.

Irene received a lot of attention as the first woman Oneida leader. "I got letters from all over, and got a lot of publicity. I don't think the men liked it much," she told her niece. The next year, she narrowly lost to Norbert Hill. "I have no regrets," she said.

On April 20, 1963, the Oneida Business Committee, chaired by Julius Danforth and with Irene's help, passed a tribal ordinance establishing the Oneida Housing Authority. It was the first Indian housing project of its kind in the state. Two months later, on June 21, 1963, the Oneida Housing Authority held its first organizational meeting. The meeting took place at the Holy Apostles Parish Hall in Oneida with Artley Skenandore Sr. presiding as chairman of the authority. The other four board members were Norbert Hill Sr., Ruth Baird, Oscar Archiquette, and Vivian DeCoteau. As part of the Oneida Housing Authority's efforts, the tribe's Business Committee, with Irene Moore as chair, Althea Schuyler as treasurer, Eva Danforth as secretary, and Lee Gordon McLester II as vice chair, bought land from the Episcopal Church and secured funding from the federal Housing and Urban Development (HUD) program in 1963. The first housing units, called Site I, were built near State Highway 54 and Duck Creek. Single-family homes were later built at Site II, the former Civilian Conservation Corps camp.

Irene was serving on the tribal executive council when she retired from the Community Action Program in October 1975. She was honored in November as Outstanding Elder of the Oneida Community for her many years of leadership.

"I hope the youth will realize that education is one of the main things in life," she said. "You have to be able to help yourself. You can't live in the days of long ago. You have to live with people today," she said in the 1975 *Press-Gazette* interview.[2]

Following the November reception in her honor, Irene wrote an open thank-you letter in the *Kalihwisaks* (pronounced Gah-lee-wee-zocks) tribal newspaper.

"I pray to be able to live up to the kind things said about me," Irene Moore wrote.

The tribal administration building most familiar to tribal members at that time was a former schoolhouse at the intersection of Outagamie County Road H and Fish Creek Road. The intersection was known as Chicago Corners ever since the land on the northeast corner had been allotted in 1892 to tribal member Joseph C. (Chicago) Smith. Smith died in 1907 at age fifty-seven, and his heirs sold the land to new owners, who in turn sold the property in 1915 to the Seymour School District for an elementary school site. The district built a public day school there in 1917 to accommodate the growing number of non-Indian residents who were moving onto lands formerly held by tribal members. Oneida historian Loretta Metoxen said the growth of public schools serving the reservation was part of the justification for the US government to close the Oneida Boarding School in 1919. The Seymour School District, however, closed the rural Chicago Corners school in 1968 as part of consolidation efforts. The tribe formally reacquired the property in a unique swap. In 1970, the Brown County–owned Austin Straubel Airport needed additional land for expansion of runways. A desired parcel, known as the Rose Skenandore property, was ten acres of tribal trust land adjoining the airport. So a deal was worked out to trade the tribal land near the Brown County airport for the old school site in Outagamie County. The Seymour district conveyed the property to the tribe on December 7, 1970, turning the old schoolhouse at Chicago Corners into the new tribal administration building. Chairman Purcell Powless and members of the Business Committee moved into offices there. A group of women held Oneida Head Start for preschoolers in the basement. Chicago Corners became a springboard for tribal government, Loretta said, a crossroads where much nation building occurred over the next ten years.

In 1973, a new tribal building opened that would later become the first site of Oneida Bingo. And bingo would not have started the way it did if not for that building. The Oneida Nation Memorial Building, better known as the civic center, would become a hub of activity for the community.

The civic center is located near the east bank of Duck Creek, close to the bridge where Wisconsin Highway 54 winds down into a wooded valley. It's in the heart of the Oneida reservation, set near the tribe's Site I housing project. In 1973, sixty families lived in Site I, part of the HUD project first approved in 1963.

Planning for the civic center started in 1968 as an athletic and recreational facility for residents. When it opened in 1973, Oneida tribal chairman Purcell Powless called it a much-needed facility. "They created a housing development, but there was nothing for the children to do," Powless told a *Green Bay Press-Gazette* reporter in May 1973.

The civic center had a gym with two full basketball courts, a two-room suite for doctor's visits, a beauty shop, a barber shop, a vending machine area, a kitchen with snack bar, a laundry facility, a library, a crafts room, and a wing with six offices for managers and directors. Marie Scott ran the beauty salon, offering haircuts for $1.50 and perms for $8 to $15. Elders like Maria Hinton, Amos Christjohn, and Mary Danforth taught Oneida language classes there. The building's extra office space allowed some administrators to move out of the crowded former schoolhouse at Chicago Corners; the tribal treasurer, Alma Webster, and the vice chairman, Norbert Hill Sr., were among those relocating to the civic center.

The civic center was set amid oak, white pine, and birch trees not far from Duck Creek. The gray concrete building looked pretty nice for 1970s architecture. The vertical fluted block of its exterior was repeated on inside walls and would save on painting, explained David "Sonny" King, the building's director, during a media tour of the building. "And don't forget our glass wigwam," Sonny pointed out to a reporter, looking up through the lobby's skylight, which indeed looked like a glass-sided tepee with black steel ribs.[3]

In an era known as Indian self-determination, when tribes were taking on greater responsibilities for their own welfare, the civic center building represented hope for the betterment of tribal members. For building director Sonny King, the civic center was the turf where he and his staff would fight truancy and alcohol and drug problems among Oneida youths. Sonny, a former barber in Chicago, had worked with youths since 1946. The tools he intended to use were activities like basketball, baseball, boxing, pinball, and roller-skating, many of which were offered at the civic center. Sonny also encouraged young people, including his own kids, to play golf. He played guitar and taught his kids to play, too. His sons, Harlan, Tim, and Conrad, learned to play country, blues, and rock in Oneida bands.

"There isn't much for these kids to do in a small community except be on the streets and drink. There are just a few activities," Tony Skenandore, athletics director of the civic center and one of Sonny's staff members, told a newspaper at the time.[4]

The building itself cost $388,000, paid with grants from HUD, the Economic Development Administration, and the Wisconsin Division of Library Services. Some foundation funds were provided for Boys' Club activities. It was up to the tribe to pay for operational costs, and the tribe had no real revenue sources.

"We had no monies coming in except for grants," recalled Alma Webster, the tribal treasurer at the time. "We had this big beautiful building but didn't have money." It was soon clear that paying for the programs and upkeep would be a formidable task. Civic center staff tried fund-raising activities such as dances, athletic tournaments, and boxing matches with admission fees. They tried rummage sales, raffles, and even a baseball game with players riding donkeys. But it wasn't enough.

In late winter of 1975, Sandra Ninham sat at her desk in the small office at the civic center going through a stack of unpaid bills. She was trying to decide which to pay first. Sandy had taken a new job as assistant director of the civic center under Sonny King. She organized homemaking classes at the civic center, arranging for people to learn how to knit, crochet, sew clothes, make rugs and draperies, and cook easy one-dish meals, in addition to learning tips on consumer credit and automobile insurance.

At age thirty-two, Sandy was married, the mother of four children, and six months pregnant with her fifth child. When she wasn't caring for her kids or organizing classes, rummage sales, bazaars, or craft shows at the civic center, she was trying to pay the center's bills. And that was getting harder and harder. The tribe had no tax base and very little revenue.

"Sonny charged all that stuff," Sandy said. "He kept buying shoes, basketballs, baseballs, and bats, and I don't know where he thought the money was coming from. I'd get the bills and try to figure it out. The light bill was $426 a month. It's a lot when you don't have anything.

"We had the gym and the lockers and tried to tell the men they had to pay a membership fee, like twenty-five dollars, to use the lockers," she continued. "They wouldn't. So that was no way to make money."

Sandy always talked over her money problems with the tribal treasurer, Alma Webster, whose office was in the same wing of the civic center. Alma was thirty-six and the mother of two girls and a boy. She loved working with numbers and playing puzzles. And she loved playing bingo. She had recently returned from visiting her sister in Lansing, Michigan, where they had gone to a VFW bingo game, when she came up with an idea about how to make money.

Bingo, Alma thought. "That's what we should do," she told Sandy.

Sandy didn't know much about bingo. She had never played the game, but she had good people skills and loved organizing events for kids and the elderly. They decided to pursue the idea.

"Bingo was all Alma's idea," Sandy said during one of our interviews. "She was the one with the lightbulb."

Alma teasingly scowled back: "She always blames me."

The seed of an idea was planted. But getting a bingo game to actually sprout in Oneida would take another year and a half and the combined efforts of many other people. Several times, it appeared it might never take root at all.

Sandy and Alma didn't take credit for starting bingo. They said it took a group effort by many women to get bingo started.

It's quite possible several women were organizing private bingo games in Oneida in the early 1970s to raise money for certain causes and benefits. After all, bingo was big entertainment back then. It was probably being played in Oneida by individuals at home parties or church basements as fund-raisers. Efforts by all these women served to inspire Alma and Sandy. The bingo game I focused on was the one conducted by the tribe for the benefit of the entire tribe. This new bingo operation would be different from previous games. Oneida Bingo would be created as a nationalized enterprise under a tribal-authorized ordinance. Other Oneida women who pushed for a new nursing home and health center were also looking for supplemental funding sources, too. Anna John, Audrey Doxtator, and Priscilla "Budgy" Manders were involved in starting those facilities. While some groups of women competed with one another and didn't always get along, tribal bingo would give them a united purpose. Their efforts converged at the civic center. So it's likely Oneida Bingo was born of many mothers. I also learned that the women couldn't have started it without help from the men. Hundreds of people were responsible for working hard as volunteers in the early days to build it into a success. I'm sorry I can't name them all.

To gain some understanding of bingo itself, I decided to look deeper into the game's history.

Modern bingo is a descendant of an Italian lottery game called lotto. Its use can be traced to 1530. Lotto spread from Italy throughout Europe in the 1700s. The classic lotto game used a playing card of three horizontal and nine vertical rows. Each lotto card was different. A caller would draw from ninety chips in a cloth bag, and players would cover the number if it appeared on their card. The first player to cover a horizontal row won.

The United States has a long history of gambling and lottery-type games, ranging from periods of prohibition to regulation. In colonial America, playing the lottery became a civic responsibility.[5] Libraries and some Ivy League universities were financed in part with lotteries. In 1776, lotteries were authorized as a way to raise money for the Continental Army and to help finance the Revolutionary War. George Washington prohibited his soldiers from gambling in camp, yet he lent his support to specific lotteries for public works projects.

Lotto's evolution into modern American bingo dates to the 1920s by several different promoters. Like the board game Monopoly, bingo grew during the hard times of the Great Depression. After the 1929 stock market crash, legalized gambling was seen as a way to stimulate the economy.

The steel-mill working-class city of Pittsburgh claims to be the home of bingo. Hugh J. Ward ran bingo games at Pittsburgh carnivals in the 1920s, took it nationwide in 1924, and wrote a book of rules on the game in 1933.[6]

Another developer at the time was a New York toy salesman named Edwin S. Lowe. (Some sources also list him as Edmund Lowe or Erwin Lowe.)

Lowe was driving late one night in December 1929 near Atlanta, Georgia, when he saw the lights of a country festival. All of the carnival booths were closed except for one, which was packed with people. The game being played was a version of lotto called beano. When someone filled a line on his or her card from numbers drawn, the winner got a Kewpie doll. Lowe tried to play the game but recalled later he couldn't get a seat. The players seemed addicted to the game. The pitchman finally closed at 3 a.m. and had to chase them out, Lowe said.[7]

After locking up, the pitchman told Lowe he had run across a game called lotto while traveling with a carnival in Germany the year before. He made a few changes in the play, renamed it beano, and brought it to the carnival circuit. Back in New York, Lowe made his own adjustments. He put together rubber stamps, cardboard, and dried beans for a game among friends at his apartment. During one session, Lowe noticed one player becoming more excited as beans covered her card. When her final number was called and she won, she jumped up and instead of shouting "Beano," stuttered "B-b-bingo!"[8]

Lowe's first game came in two versions: a twelve-card set for a dollar, and a twenty-four-card set for two dollars. It was an immediate hit. Several months later, however, a priest from Wilkes-Barre, Pennsylvania approached Lowe about a problem. The church was using Lowe's two-dollar game as a fund-raiser but found there were too many duplicate winners. Lowe then contracted with a retired mathematician to develop six thousand new bingo cards with nonrepeating number groups. By 1934, there were ten thousand bingo games being played each week nationwide and Lowe had a thousand employees printing cards to meet demand.[9]

The modern bingo card contains five rows of five spaces each, with each space printed with a number from 1 to 75, except the center space, which is marked free.

Bingo spread from the East Coast to the West Coast. Gaming entrepreneur Bill Harrah recounted that his father, John, an attorney, had moved his family from Iowa to Los Angeles in 1930 and opened a bingo hall in Venice, California. Bill, a student at the University of California at Los Angeles, bought out his father's operation in 1933. For his part, Bill took a trip to Reno in 1937, bought a bingo hall there, and sold the Venice operation. He opened his first casino in Reno in 1946 with bingo profits. "Any bingo player knows when there's a 'small' crowd, the pots are just the same, you have a better chance, so they rush in and play," Harrah said in 1977, shortly before his death.[10]

Massachusetts decriminalized bingo in 1931 as a way to help charities raise money. Conversely, Wisconsin's Supreme Court ruled in 1940 that bingo was an illegal lottery regardless of whether proceeds were used for public benefit. However, sheriffs and police in Wisconsin were reluctant to enforce the law due to the popularity of low-stakes bingo for charitable purposes. By the 1950s, bingo was legal in eleven states (Wisconsin excluded). At that time, merchants were allowed to use games of chance in promotional contests to boost profits. Many people said charities should be allowed to do the same with bingo.

Given the extreme popularity of bingo across the country, it's not surprising the Oneida Nation of Wisconsin wasn't the first Indian tribe to hit on the idea of using bingo as a fund-raiser. The Penobscot Indian Tribe opened its high-stakes bingo hall on Indian Island in Old Town, Maine, in 1973. The tribe claims it was the first commercial gambling operation on an Indian reservation in the United States. Bingo is held there to this day, one weekend every six weeks, and draws about twelve hundred people from all over the Northeast.

Before 1973, bingo was still technically illegal in Wisconsin under the lottery prohibition in the state's constitution, but that didn't stop Green Bay. In the early 1970s, bingo games were being sponsored there primarily through Catholic church organizations. Green Bay is predominantly Catholic, having been settled by immigrants of French, German, Belgian, Polish, Irish, and Dutch heritage.[11] As immigrants moved in, they formed their own ethnic parishes: Germans at St. Mary (now St. Francis Xavier Cathedral), Dutch at St. Willebrord, Irish at St. Patrick, Belgians at Ss. Peter and Paul, and Polish at St. Mary of the Angels. St. Norbert College in De Pere was founded in 1898 by a Dutch immigrant priest, Abbot Bernard Pennings. Catholic influence pervaded the community. But you didn't have to be Catholic to enjoy attending parish picnics, Friday perch fry dinners, or bingo games in Green Bay.

I later interviewed Mary Mullin, who in 1970 was a young mother from the Green Bay suburb of Ashwaubenon. She told me her priest at Nativity of Our Lord Catholic Church asked her to start a bingo game to help finance a new roof, which cost about seventy-five thousand dollars at the time. "In the first year, we raised thirty thousand dollars," said Mullin, who later became a state bingo inspector and served as Ashwaubenon village trustee.

Although technically illegal, Wisconsin bingo games at that time were permitted because payment by players was ostensibly in the form of a voluntary donation. That was about to change. Wisconsin voters approved a statewide referendum on April 3, 1973, to legalize bingo. The vote amended the state constitution to permit bingo for charitable or nonprofit groups, provided that all revenue would go to the licensed organizations and that no salaries, fees, or profits would be paid to other organizations or people. Charities were limited in individual jackpots and total prizes per session. In return, the state would get its share of bingo proceeds through a 2 percent gross receipts tax, 4 percent sales tax, ten-dollar license fee for each event, and annual fee of five dollars for each member responsible for supervising the games. That amounted to about a 7 percent take for the state.

Other Midwest states like Illinois and Michigan had already legalized bingo. Green Bay–area residents favored legalizing bingo as well. Many people felt it was a way for the elderly to stay involved socially and have fun. One senior, Mrs. Leona Basten, enjoyed playing bingo at Nativity of Our Lord Catholic Church in Ashwaubenon along with other retired friends. "Even if you don't win, you like to go out and socialize, to see other people," she told a *Green Bay Press-Gazette* reporter. In a story published the week before the 1973 spring election, she said she wanted to see bingo legalized. "My stars, life itself is a little gamble more than a little bingo game," Basten said.[12]

People she knew were willing to travel far to play bingo. Before local groups offered bingo, her friends used to drive to Michigan's Upper Peninsula to play. Her sister in Milwaukee traveled to Illinois to play.

Bingo also was a way for private Catholic schools like Green Bay Premontre High School to raise money to defray the school's deficit. The Premontre Parents Association began holding bingo games in October 1972, twice a month on Wednesday nights. Harold Keigl, one of the workers at the Premontre games, said bingo was fun for players and a boon for fundraising. He told the *Press-Gazette* that bingo had raised several thousand dollars for the school.

Jerome Quinn, a state assembly legislator who supported the bingo amendment, said he could see no harm in bingo as long as it was properly supervised. If it led to professional gamblers coming into Wisconsin for illegal operation, then legislators could reevaluate the bingo law, he said. "But I doubt this would happen because under the proposed law all bingo games must be licensed by the state," he told the *Press-Gazette*.

Local law enforcement officials expressed caution about opening the door to gambling. Donald Zuidmulder, who was Brown County district attorney in 1973, was quoted in the *Press-Gazette* as saying he was generally opposed to gambling because it could lead to social problems, "just like drinking creates a lot of social problems." But he felt assured that with approval of the bingo referendum, the state would take steps to carefully license and regulate the games. "On that basis, it overcomes my general reservation on gambling," Zuidmulder said in the 1973 article.[13]

On the Oneida Indian Reservation, less than two years later, Alma Webster and Sandy Ninham were thinking about starting a bingo game to help pay the civic center's bills. Other groups were doing it to raise money, why not the tribe? But where do you start?

"We didn't have any idea how to run bingo," Alma recalled. She and Pat Misikin and Kate Stevens, two other Oneida women, went to the Veterans of Foreign Wars post in De Pere to study how they played bingo games there. "That's what we based it on, the way they played," Alma said. "We'd sit there and see how many numbers it would [take for bingo to] go in," Alma said.

Sandy said the group's research of other bingo halls helped them get a start. "No one gave us approval to do it. We just did it," she said.

By March 1975, word of bingo coming to the Oneida civic center was being talked up in the Oneida tribal newspaper, the *Kalihwisaks*. A small item in the March 7, 1975, issue stated that proceeds from a rummage sale held March 2 would be used to buy prizes for a bingo game. The date of the bingo game would be announced soon, the newspaper said.

As late winter melted away in Wisconsin on a sunny March day in 1975, Alma and Sandy drove down US 41 to Oshkosh. They had found a store where they were told they could buy bingo supplies for their first game.

Alma drove as Sandy tried to resist sleep. "The sun was shining and I was pregnant with Matthew," Sandy recalled. "I remember I had on a green top with a gold turtleneck underneath. I was so sleepy."

In Oshkosh, they entered the store with a list of what they needed: bingo cards, balls with bingo letters and numbers on them, and a revolving cage to pick the balls. The store clerk piled the stuff on the counter and then asked them for their Wisconsin Bingo Control Board license number.

What number? What license? "Of course we didn't have one," Sandy said. "We tried to convince him we were a tribe and didn't need one. But he wouldn't sell it to us. So we left." The supplier had little choice. The bingo control law stated that licensed suppliers were prohibited from selling to anyone without a state bingo license. A supplier who violated the law could lose his license.

The two women went home empty-handed. The ride back was discouraging. "I could have just died when we didn't get that number the first time," Sandy said. "It would have been easy to think, we're just Indians; we can't do this. But we never gave up. We always talked about doing this."

Notes

1. Irene Moore, interview with niece Madelyn Genskow, July 5, 1976, Seymour, WI.
2. "Indian Leader Cited," *Green Bay Press-Gazette*, November 28, 1975.
3. "Much-Needed Oneida Center Ready," *Green Bay Press-Gazette*, May 25, 1973.
4. "Oneida's Sonny King Focuses on Activity for Youngsters," *Green Bay Press-Gazette*, November 3, 1974.
5. Charles T. Clotfelter and Philip J. Cook, *Selling Hope: State Lotteries in America* (Cambridge, MA: Harvard University Press, 1989).
6. "Bingo: It's a Money-Maker and a Way of Life," *Pittsburgh Post-Gazette*, April 13, 2003.
7. Roger Snowden, *Gambling Times Guide to Bingo* (Lyle Stuart, 1986).
8. Ibid.
9. Ibid.

10. Ibid.

11. The Association of Religious Data Archives estimated the Catholic population in Green Bay at more than 70 percent.

12. "Opinion in County Tends to Favor Legal Bingo," *Green Bay Press-Gazette,* April 1, 1973.

13. Ibid. Donald Zuidmulder was later elected judge and chief judge of Brown County Circuit Court.

CHAPTER 3

Oneida Stories: From Termination to Determination

I COULD find no mention of bingo again for a whole year in the *Kalihwisaks*, the Oneida tribal newspaper. There was the brief mention in the March 7, 1975, issue about proceeds from a March 2 rummage sale intended for an upcoming bingo game, but nothing further until the following March. That's when the *Kalihwisaks* ran a note in the March 5, 1976, issue saying there would be no bingo games until a license was obtained.

The hiatus of bingo news aside, there was plenty worth reading about in Oneida in the late 1970s. I spent about a month, off and on, reading back copies of the *Kalihwisaks* at the Oneida Cultural Heritage Department.

The department is housed in a converted two-story family residence built in the 1970s. The tribe acquired the property near Highway 54 and Hillcrest Road in the 1990s. I entered a receptionist area in the foyer where genealogist Beverly Skenandore worked. In a room opening to the right, tribal historian Loretta Metoxen was surrounded by shelves of books and maps. Stairs straight ahead from the foyer led to second-floor bedrooms that were converted to offices. The area to the left of the foyer opened to a large U-shaped kitchen and dining room with tables set in a semicircle. The department kept boxes of *Kalihwisaks* copies since the early 1970s, and for days I'd sit near the communal kitchen area looking over records and reading descriptions of what was happening in the community three decades earlier.

The name *Kalihwisaks* means "She Looks for News." Back in the 1970s, the *Kalihwisaks* was really more of a newsletter of stapled typewritten pages than a traditional newspaper. (An earlier tribal newsletter, called *The Scout*, had been started in the 1960s by Woodrow Webster, Lee Gordon McLester

II, and Artley Skenandore Sr.) In the late 1970s, the *Kalihwisaks* was published every other week. It was usually about ten typewritten pages of 8.5-by-14-inch paper stapled together. Oneida youths received five dollars if their artwork was picked for the cover. The *Kalihwisaks* office was in Room 19 in the Sacred Heart Center. The editor at the time, Betty Ritchie, and the reporter, Debbie House, did most of the work themselves, running off copies on a tabletop mimeograph machine in the office and dropping off new copies at area offices and stores.

Copies of the *Kalihwisaks* were mailed to subscribers and also were available for ten cents each at the Chicago Corners tribal building; Maas's Grocery at Fish Creek Road and Outagamie County Road H; Morgan's Store and Schroeder's Market on Service Road; and the Oneida Tribal Development Corporation and Community Action Program offices in Oneida and Green Bay. Circulation was on the rise, growing from 200 to 490 between February and December 1975.

"Hopefully we'll soon publish a more conventional looking paper," Ritchie wrote in the January 9, 1976, edition. The *Kalihwisaks* today is a full-sized newspaper and is mailed to all tribal members.

Issues carried typical community news: birth and death notices, recipes, and folk remedies. "To make Indian salve, boil wormwood, strain, add lard, and boil until the water's out. It's good for sore throats and rheumatism," according to Elizabeth Huff as told to Tillie Baird, who interviewed community members during the Depression-era Oneida Language and Folklore Project.

The paper also provided updates on people in the community. The March 7, 1975, *Kalihwisaks*, for example, reported that John Hill, age twenty-two, son of Minnie Hill, arrived home after serving three years in the navy and was "free to rejoin his family." Teenager Dennis Danforth advanced in a national boxing tournament until he injured his hand.

Charlie Hill, son of Norbert and Eileen Hill, was a promising standup comic at the Palomino Club and Two Dollar Bills in Los Angeles, according to the February 20, 1976, *Kalihwisaks*, in an article reprinted from a California newspaper. Charlie, a former UW–Madison student, was trying out his Henry Youngblood routine on audiences: "My horse shot himself last night. So I went out this morning and broke one of his legs."

Charlie sharpened his routines at the Comedy Store in L.A. and began to use humor the way his dad, Norbert, threw jabs as a young boxer. In

1977, he appeared on *The Richard Pryor Show* and told the audience he was an Oneida from Wisconsin: "We used to be from New York, but we had real estate problems." Charlie said it was his dream that one day he would win an award for acting, "and then refuse it because of the mistreatment of Marlon Brando." In September 1978, he made it onto Johnny Carson's *Tonight Show.* "They call us Vanishing Americans. But when was the last time you saw a Pilgrim?" he said. Charlie lived in Los Angeles, making his living by writing for comedy shows, though he regularly returned to Wisconsin each year to do standup.

Another *Kalihwisaks* issue reported that someone vandalized the Holy Apostles parish hall and tipped over cemetery stones. Someone broke into the *Kalihwisaks* office and took eighteen dollars. A woodstove caused a fire that burned down a couple's home one winter. An eighteen-year-old Oneida man was killed in a car crash.

The September 3, 1976, issue reported that Loretta Ellis married Floyd Metoxen, forming a combined family of thirteen kids from ages seven to twenty-three. A reception for two hundred guests was held at the Swan Club in De Pere.

In the October 29, 1976, issue of *Kalihwisaks*, in a note titled "The Indian Way," Mrs. Prudence Doxtator wrote that she wished to thank all the hardworking McLester men who put the roofing on her house, as well as the women who provided food during a work bee.

Leafing through the pages of the tribal newsletter, I found myself caught up in the rhythm of life and cycle of nature. It was like looking out your back window and seeing, over the course of an hour, all four seasons come and go.

According to the *Kalihwisaks*, 1977 was a particularly frigid winter, as Oneida Head Start was closed for six days in January due to severe cold weather. Each issue of the newspaper offered a teachable phrase in the Oneida language appropriate to the season. The January 19, 1979, issue noted a lot of people in Oneida said: "My car wouldn't start." Old, beat-up cars and trucks, known as "rez runners," were often on the road long past their trade-in value. Kids used flattened cardboard boxes for sleds. Dress in layers, the paper advised, and watch that your kids don't sled on hills next to highways. An Iroquois winter tradition was to play snow snake, a game in which people try to throw a long wooden pole the farthest down a trench hollowed out of the snow.

In late winter, ice started breaking up in Duck Creek, so fish were moving upstream. Fishermen were advised to get their gill nets ready. People fished for suckers in Duck Creek back then, and I found recipes for sucker head soup. Hudson Doxtator predicted an early spring because he saw a caterpillar walking on snow, according to the March 14, 1980, issue.

Late winter also is maple syrup time. The traditional maple festival honors the return of spring; people thank the Creator for having survived another winter. Volunteers collected sap from maples in the woods around Sacred Heart Center, the March 28, 1980, *Kalihwisaks* reported. When you boil down the sap, you have *w'ahta ohses* (maple syrup), the paper said.

In late May or June, the strawberry festival celebrates the return of wild strawberries. It also marks the traditional time to plant beans and corn.

The Oneida tribe holds its annual powwow on the July Fourth holiday on a scenic hillside behind the Sacred Heart Center. The hillside is terraced down to a lacrosse field and pond set amid woods close to Duck Creek. The powwow kicks off with a parade down the West Service Road to Site I and back up the hill to the powwow grounds. An honor guard of military veterans leads the parade, followed by local floats, kids on bikes, fire trucks, drummers in the back of a pickup truck, people on horseback, and Miss Oneida waving from a convertible.

In early August, the green corn festival was held when the corn was high. People made a dish of green corn called *okahslotha*. New corn or green corn before it's ripe is called *on^stase*, the tribal newspaper said.

The October 29, 1976, issue urged young people to sign up for a big buck contest for one dollar at the civic center. The top hunter would get a trophy for the largest male deer shot that year.

During the fall harvest, all vegetables would be put away for winter. The tribe's Iroquois Farms' six-acre garden yielded spinach, tomatoes, beets, potatoes, and sweet corn. Tribal members got the idea in 1976 to start a cannery, a food-processing facility meant to train people how to become food self-reliant. The tribe received a grant to buy cannery equipment in 1977 and worked with the Green Bay Catholic Diocese to lease space in the basement of Sacred Heart Center. The cannery was dedicated in 1978 and remains there today. The cannery became the foundation of the Tsyunhehkwa program and was meant to pass on the knowledge of making traditional food, including cornbread and corn soup. The cannery is open to the public.

Harvest and Thanksgiving meals were offered each November to the community at Holy Apostles parish hall and at Oneida United Methodist Church. Menu items included turkey, venison, squash, corn soup, potatoes, wild rice, and pumpkins. "It tastes good" translates in Oneida as *ya we'ku* (pronounced ya-way-goo), the November 19, 1977, *Kalihwisaks* noted.

The tribal newspaper in late December said Oneida children would celebrate Hoyan (meaning "another"), the traditional New Year's celebration, by going door-to-door to receive homemade doughnuts on January 1. Many Oneida families prepared doughnuts and apples for the kids.

It was again late December when I sat at the kitchen counter reading those old accounts of Oneida from more than thirty years earlier. During that winter week, I overheard conversations around me in the longhouse office. Cultural adviser Bob Brown met with families who wanted to arrange traditional ceremonies. Randy Cornelius held Oneida language classes at noon around the semicircle of tables in what had been a dining room. Michelle Danforth, Charlie Doxtater, and Nic Reynolds were working on an animated video language lesson teaching people to say *shekoli* (pronounced say-go'-lee), or "hello."

Staff members came in during breaks to get coffee or fix themselves toast or a bowl of cereal. Loretta Metoxen mentioned she would be making her traditional Hoyan doughnuts in the kitchen again on New Year's Day for the community. She usually made about twenty-four dozen throughout the day for visitors.

Doughnuts? I could go for some doughnuts, I thought to myself. I would say, *Ya we'ku*.

After continued searching, I found one clue why the news on bingo had stopped after March 1975. Sandy Ninham had more pressing concerns at the moment than bingo. The May 2, 1975, issue of *Kalihwisaks* noted that she was on leave from her job at the civic center to have her baby and would be returning in late summer. Sharon (House) Weasel took over Sandy's job as assistant director in her absence. Sandy's fifth child and third son, Matthew, was born a few weeks later. Sandy worked from home that summer selling pots and pans and held a rummage sale at her home on Florist

Drive, while her husband, Leland, worked at Green Bay Packaging's paper mill. She returned to her job in August as assistant director of the civic center and shared the job part-time with Sharon. They started scheduling arts and crafts, needlepoint, rug-making, and sewing classes.

Maintenance expenses at the civic center remained an ongoing problem. The July 11, 1975, *Kalihwisaks* noted that profits from an arts and crafts sale "hopefully . . . will take care of some of the upkeep." A dance at Schuyler's Hall on August 8 raised money to buy uniforms for Babe Ruth League players.

Other exciting things were happening in Oneida, though bingo wasn't among them. The Oneida post office, which had been located inside Schroeder's Market on Service Road for many years, was moving into its own building at Site I. Excavation started in October 1975 for the new post office building. The seven-thousand-square-foot building would have room for the Indian Action Program and an arts and crafts center. Similar to the nearby civic center, it was built with fluted concrete block. The new post office building would be named for the late Oscar Archiquette.

Oscar Archiquette was born June 15, 1901, in Oneida. His paternal grandparents emigrated from Oneida Castle, New York. His father, John Archiquette, volunteered in the Civil War in 1861 at age fourteen, later served as captain of the Indian police force, and ran a farm two miles south of the Episcopal stone church. His parents, John and Christine, were Christian. Oscar grew up speaking only Oneida. He learned English at the Oneida mission school. He admittedly floundered around the country as a young man, though he returned to Oneida and worked diligently to reorganize the nation during the New Deal. He became Oneida tribal president under a short-lived state charter in 1934–1935. After the tribe voted for reorganization under federal charter, Oscar Archiquette served one-year terms as tribal vice chairman eight times over three decades. He participated in the New Deal–era Works Progress Administration's Oneida Language and Folklore Project chronicling the lives of the Oneida in their own words. In the 1950s, Oscar Archiquette was among a group of Oneida who successfully fought efforts to terminate the tribe. He was instrumental in recording and transcribing Oneida language as a learning tool for future generations. He taught Oneida language at Highview School on Florist Drive to anyone who wanted to learn. He died at age seventy in Green Bay on December 25, 1971, after a short illness.

Tribal historian Loretta Metoxen told me that in 1967, Oscar Archiquette and Norbert Hill Sr. visited her twice to try to get her to run for the Business Committee. "I told them no the first time," she said. She was Loretta Ellis back then, raising six kids on her own in a cabin with no running water. Finally, she relented and was elected secretary. Working alongside her were Purcell Powless, who had been elected chairman; Oscar Archiquette, vice chairman; and Joy Ninham, treasurer. Loretta served in various positions on the council until 1996.

Loretta said Oscar Archiquette's life spanned a huge era. He grew up as the reservation was being dismantled under allotment, and he played a role in Oneida politics in the New Deal reorganization. He fought termination and lived to see self-determination policies enacted. Traditional Oneida language and culture never disappeared entirely, Loretta said. While many Oneida attended Christian churches by day, they also met in homes at night to keep the old traditions alive. "This was told to me by Oscar Archiquette," Loretta recalled.

In the 1960s, federal Great Society programs under President Lyndon B. Johnson allowed tribal leaders to apply to federal agencies for grants and to administer programs themselves. The 1964 Economic Opportunity Act was meant to fight poverty, including on the reservation. Loretta told me the Community Action Program assisted Oneida elders in their homes and neighborhood youth programs.

In 1968, President Johnson identified the new goal of federal Indian policy as one of "partnership and self-help," providing Indians an opportunity to remain in their homelands or move if they chose. But the new policy didn't end when the Democrat Johnson left the White House in 1969. Purcell Powless, Oneida tribal chair from 1967 to 1990, said in a video interview that "it was Nixon and the Republicans who helped Indians the most."[1]

In 1970, President Richard Nixon articulated a new self-determination policy, calling for an end to termination and urging Congress to return control of federal Indian programs to tribes. In his July 8, 1970, Special Message on Indian Affairs, Nixon said, "It is long past time that the Indian policies of the federal government began to recognize and build upon the capacities and insights of the Indian people. Both as a matter of justice and as a matter of enlightened social policy, we must begin to act on the basis of what the Indians themselves have long been telling us. The time has come to break decisively with the past and to create the conditions for a new era in which the Indian future is determined by Indian acts and Indian decisions."

The shift in policy broke the BIA's monopoly on administering programs and enabled the tribes to develop ties with a wide range of federal agencies. The Indian Self-Determination and Education Assistance Act, passed by Congress in 1975, provided more Indian control of schools that educated Indian kids. The 1975 act amended the Johnson-O'Malley Act of 1934, in which the Department of the Interior contracted with school districts that taught Indian children. The Wisconsin Oneida tribe was among 370 Indian nations to contract for services in the first five years.[2]

Also in 1975, Congress approved a major investigation of the BIA as part of the American Indian Policy Review Commission Act. The policy review act came in response to recent social upheavals in Indian country: the Indian takeover of Alcatraz Island in 1969; the march on Washington, DC, and takeover of BIA headquarters in 1972; and the Indian occupation of Wounded Knee in 1973.

The panel, also known as the Abourezk Commission, was created to study the historical and legal status of Indian nations and recommend new legislation. Senator James Abourezk, a Democrat from South Dakota and chair of the Senate Select Committee on Indian Affairs, sponsored the act. Largely staffed by Indians and headed by Ernest Stevens Sr., a charismatic leader and Wisconsin Oneida tribal member, the commission investigated such topics as trust responsibilities, tribal government, federal administration, health care, and education.[3] An overriding theme in the final report was greater recognition of tribal sovereignty.

These two acts challenged the overbearing colonial relationship that had existed between the federal government and Indian nations and provided for a greater tribal voice in decision making, according to Laurence M. Hauptman's introduction to *A Nation within a Nation: Voices of the Oneidas in Wisconsin*. The two acts did not create sovereignty in the minds of the Wisconsin Oneida, however. They merely reinforced what the Oneida had always known they were: a sovereign nation, Hauptman wrote.

Reading through the old *Kalihwisaks* newsletters, I could sense growing optimism in the Oneida community as 1976 started:

- Tribal officials and Bishop Aloysius John Wycislo were discussing future uses of the Sacred Heart Center on Seminary Road. Loretta Metoxen, a Business Committee member at the time, was among tribal leaders who met weekly with the bishop over tea to negotiate the tribe resuming control of the property. It had been the site of the Oneida Boarding School for tribal youths from 1893 to 1919. The ninety-acre property included thirty-five acres of woods. The buildings included thirteen classrooms, eighteen living suites, a gym, a cafeteria, a library, and a lounge. The current brick structure was built in 1954 as a boarding school for young men studying for the priesthood. But fewer men were entering the priesthood, so the diocese converted it into a coed Catholic high school. The diocese closed the school in 1976 and leased empty space to community groups. The Oneida tribe housed its child care, Head Start, and *Kalihwisaks* offices there. The talk in Oneida was that it could become a tribal facility, the *Kalihwisaks* said.
- Some Oneida were returning to the reservation as the tribe obtained funds to reacquire lands lost after the allotment. The Ernest Stevens family, which had been living in Washington, DC, where Ernest Sr. headed the American Indian Policy Review Commission, was planning to move back to Oneida in 1976 "because of his interest in his people acquiring more land for the Oneida tribe," the *Kalihwisaks* reported.[4]
- In March 1976, the tribe received the go-ahead to build a fifty-bed nursing home for Oneida elderly. Anna John, for whom the nursing home was later named, pushed hard to get the $1.07 million project financed, primarily through a federal Hill-Burton grant. The Methodist Church and Johnson Wax Foundation donated funds. Oneida voters also approved allocating funds for the nursing home from a trust fund set up from annual payments from the United States as part of the Treaty of Canandaigua.
- The tribe received a $106,000 grant to build a bark-covered longhouse, a replica of the traditional Iroquois multifamily dwelling. It would be located at the site of what would become a tribal museum planned near Outagamie County roads E and EE. The Oneida tribe added an

additional one hundred thousand dollars toward construction of the museum.

• The *Kalihwisaks* was becoming a vital communication link in the community, editor Betty Ritchie told readers in 1976.

An editorial in the April 2, 1976, issue enthused: "It's not all gloom and doom in Oneida. This could not have been accomplished without each person working together towards a common goal, a better life for all members of the community." The editorial gave credit to federal assistance "and tribal members working together to obtain it." The Oneida Nation Memorial Building is a hub of the community, health services, housing, education, and "our very own 50-bed nursing home soon to be built."

The editorial continued: "Our ancestors could only dream of such things, now they are a reality. Not because one or two people wanted or thought we needed more services but because we joined hands and went forth as one body to obtain these programs."

That was the mood of the time, according to the *Kalihwisaks* editorial. And bingo as a tribal enterprise hadn't even started. It was still a dream.

Alma Webster and Sandy Ninham continued to work their day jobs at the civic center—Alma as tribal treasurer and Sandy as facility assistant director—over the winter of 1975–1976 while still pursuing the idea of bingo. The unsuccessful supply run to Oshkosh was a learning experience. They knew they needed help from others in the tribe to get bingo going, and they leaned heavily on Norbert Hill Sr., the tribal vice chairman whose office also was in the civic center. Tom Parins Sr., a Green Bay lawyer who had provided pro bono legal help to the Oneida tribe in the 1970s, said Norbert came to his office with a legal question soon after bingo started. "He wanted to know if it was legal for the Oneida tribe to hold its own bingo," Tom recalled. When asked what would be done with the profits, Norbert said proceeds would provide tribal services, similar to how the churches and charities were using bingo profits. "The government won't look at the tribe the same way it looks at the church. It's not going to be easy. There's a good chance you'll face a fight," Tom recalled telling Norbert.

"Tom, I've got some women behind this thing and I wouldn't want to be the guy who has to try to shut them down," Norbert replied.

Norbert, age sixty-four at the time, helped Alma and Sandy's efforts by drawing on decades of experience in tribal government. His assistant,

Audrey Doxtator, who had worked to get the Oneida Community Health Center built, also helped.

"He was so sympathetic when we came back from the trip to Oshkosh. He got involved and so did Audrey," Sandy said. At Norbert Hill's direction, Audrey wrote letters to the state inquiring about rules for obtaining a bingo license.

Norbert Hill was dedicated to helping his people and had an endless supply of ideas, according to an essay written by his family. He was born in 1912 in Oneida, the third of six children of Dr. Lily Rosa Minoka and Abram Charles Hill. His father died in 1916, when Norbert was four. His mother, one of the first female physicians in the country, was his greatest inspiration and influence, the essay said. His mom ran a "kitchen clinic" in Oneida while raising six kids. Norbert was a lifelong learner, though he did not follow the traditional path of education.

"Going to school and getting an education were two different things and they didn't always happen at the same time," Norbert often quoted his mother as saying. His love of adventure prompted him to drop out of high school in De Pere at age fourteen and enlist in the National Guard in 1926. He was stationed at Wisconsin's Camp McCoy for two years before his superiors verified his age and told him to return to school. A strong athlete, he played football at Green Bay West High School and in 1931 became the first Indian to score a touchdown against crosstown rival Green Bay East High School. He later hopped trains and visited Indian tribes out West. In 1934 he became Golden Gloves champion with sixty wins and four losses. Though just shy of six feet, he was quick on his feet and mastered a devastating counterpunch. His boxing career became a metaphor that would guide his life, said the essay.[5]

Norbert worked as a machinist for Ford Motor Co. in Detroit in the 1930s, became an activist in labor unions and community groups, and helped start the North American Indian Club. With a desire to serve his country, he joined the Navy Seabees in 1942 and served for thirty-eight months in the Aleutian Islands and Hawaii. After the war, he returned to Detroit and married Eileen Johnson, a Cree from Alberta, Canada. They raised six children: Barbara, Norbert Jr., Rosa, Charles, Richard (Rick), and James. Norbert completed vocational courses as a machinist under the GI Bill.

The family moved back to Oneida in 1962 and Norbert served as Oneida tribal chair from 1964 to 1967. In 1970, at age sixty-two, he attended the University of Wisconsin–Green Bay, where he took courses in urban planning and economics. It was during his work organizing and commanding a Michigan VFW post years earlier that he learned how bingo could be used as an economic development tool. As Oneida tribal vice chairman in the mid-1970s, he became instrumental in helping bingo become an economic force for his own tribe.[6] "Norb Hill found us someone in Chicago to sell us bingo supplies," Sandy told me. The supplier wouldn't require them to have a Wisconsin Bingo Control license, and this time, Sandy and Alma didn't go alone on the supply run.

Business Committee member Mark Powless, son of Lois and John Powless and grandson of Irene Moore, drove, accompanied by two other Oneida moms—Lillian King, a daughter of Irene Moore, and Pat Misikin. Pat and Alma played bingo together, and as a teenager, Sandy had babysat Lillian's children. Lillian was another avid bingo player.

"We went to a dumpy part of town, a dirty warehouse office in a scary part of town," Sandy said about the trip to Chicago. "Mark was the only man with us."

"We brought enough supplies back to get us started," Alma added.

The women lacked the authorization to start, however. It was not clear if state rules would apply to the tribe, and they still had not obtained the license.

Meanwhile, the *Kalihwisaks* reported June 11, 1976, that tribal member Francis Skenandore had been hired as a summer legal assistant for the tribe. Francis, a former machinist with a wife and two young daughters in Oneida, was a thirty-seven-year-old law student at the University of New Mexico at the time.

Francis told me one of his first tasks in the tribal law office was to craft a bingo ordinance that would be adopted by the tribe's Business Committee. Francis said pursuing a state bingo license was never the tribe's strategy. The tribe didn't need one because it was not subject to state civil laws. The tribe wouldn't have qualified as a charitable organization under state rules anyway, he said. "It was always our position that we as a sovereign nation could offer bingo pursuant to an ordinance being written. Our position was always, 'We can do this.' If there's a problem, we will defend the tribe."

Francis had studied social work at the University of Kansas but never practiced in that field. In his senior year he had an internship at Haskell Indian Junior College in Lawrence, Kansas. "It was a time of social unrest," he recalled. "There was the black movement, Chicano and Indian people were protesting, people were marching." The University of Kansas was a hotbed of politics. "During the internship at Haskell, a law student I knew told me I'd make a good lawyer." So he took the Law School Admissions Test. At that time, Gerald "Jerry" L. Hill, another Oneida, was studying to be a lawyer, too. Francis, Jerry, and Sharon (House) Cornelius would be the first Oneida to work as tribal lawyers. Previously, the tribe contracted with non-Oneida attorneys for legal help. The three Oneida were in their late thirties and early forties by the time they finished law school and passed the bar.

"We came through the '60s and '70s real strong on Indian sovereignty, proponents of Indian civil rights, self-determinism, self-governance," Francis said. "We came up during a time when tribes were beginning to exercise their sovereignty. We came in with the attitude [that] tribes have a right to self-govern. We came back to Oneida with the outlook that we can do this [bingo] as a government but we must do it as an ordinance. And we will defend it."

The bingo ordinance stated that bingo would be run as a tribal enterprise that benefited tribal people and programs. It also set limits on the amount of prizes paid.

As tribal secretary in 1976, Amelia Cornelius recalled the bingo issue coming before the tribe's Business Committee. "If the state allowed charities to offer it, then the tribe could offer it. I was all for it. Bingo was a game played at baby showers, churches, and was not at all unusual," she said.

"I remember Francis [Skenandore] bringing a draft ordinance to the committee at maybe two meetings. Nobody knew how much money bingo would make. We wanted to get enough to pay the bills. Nobody knew how greatly accepted and enjoyed it would become," Amelia told me.

While raising six kids, Amelia served as tribal secretary from 1968 through 1976. Her office at the time was at the tribal building at Chicago Corners. Her mother, Priscilla "Budgy" Manders, was involved in tribal affairs and often kept company with Anna John and Audrey Doxtator. In fact, Priscilla, Anna, and Audrey were seen together so often that chairman Purcell Powless called them the "Three Amigos," according to Audrey's son, Vern Doxtator.

Like many women in the Oneida community, Anna John volunteered at the day care housed in the basement of the tribal administration building. One winter day in about 1970, a child who arrived by bus from Site II housing came to day care wearing just rubber galoshes over bare feet. "He had no shoes or socks. Anna John took it upon herself to get in her car, drive to Seymour, and she bought that boy some shoes and socks. The roads were glare ice!" Betty Doxtator recalled.

For her part, Audrey was instrumental in starting the tribe's health center, and Priscilla was a licensed practical nurse. The three women worked together on starting a tribal nursing home in Oneida and raising funds for its operating expenses, Amelia said. Anna John suggested that the tribe build its own nursing home. She approached Purcell about getting funding and Purcell said to just go do it, Amelia recalled.

"Anna John was feisty. She'd tell you right to your face. I didn't mind that," Purcell Powless said in a video interview.[7]

"My dad knew that it was women running the tribe and he'd go to bat for them," said Purcell's daughter, Bobbi (Powless) Webster. "In retrospect, I think he was keeping these factions of women at bay. He had all these women coming in and telling him, 'Purcy, you've got to do something about her.' He was juggling them. That was the balance created. 'All these women, get them in one room and nothing gets accomplished,' my dad said. 'But separate them and then these two will start something and those two will start something. But you can't get them all together. Too many bosses,'" Bobbi recalled her dad saying.

Bobbi started working in the tribe's language program in 1974 for two dollars an hour. Now public relations director for the Oneida tribe, Bobbi has more than twenty-five years of experience in journalism, communications, advertising, marketing, and public relations.

"He and my mom wouldn't talk tribal business at home," she recalled. "He'd complain to me about other people. My mom said, 'He's not yelling at you, he's confiding in you.' That's when I realized I became my dad's confidante. He trusted me and told me things in confidence. It's because we worked in the same venue."

Purcell encouraged and supported the women who surrounded him, Bobbi said. "He knew they were doing things because they loved their children, loved the community."

The Oneida were in the process of building the nursing home at the same time bingo was starting. Grants financed the construction cost of the nursing home, but not furnishings such as bed linens, clocks, or curtains. Organizers needed another source of funds to help cover costs of the nursing home. Bingo would become that source.

Meanwhile, Sandy and Alma came to work at the civic center that summer, driving past workers putting up walls for the new post office as they entered Site I. Sandy organized a flea market and arts and crafts sale at the civic center. Over the summer of 1976 the bingo ordinance was approved, and by September they were ready to start bingo.

The September 17 issue of *Kalihwisaks* announced in a short item:

BINGO
Sunday, Sept. 19, 1976
Oneida Nation Memorial Building
Doors open at 4 p.m. Begin 5 p.m.
We'll see you all there.

The day of the inaugural bingo game was a typical Indian summer day in Oneida, with a daytime high reaching seventy before cooling off in the evening. Trees along Duck Creek still had green leaves and were just starting to turn into their fall gold, red, and orange. The sky was partly cloudy with a chance of rain in the air.

The gym was wearing a new look. Paula "Pogi" King, one of Sonny King's daughters, had been working high up on scaffolding for several weeks painting two murals on a wall of the gym, one a profile of an Indian chief, the other a landscape featuring the Oneida logo. Paula, an art student, had designed the murals that each stood about ten feet high.

Sandy and Alma brought their kids with them to work the first bingo game as volunteers. The moms sent the kids out with flyers to homes in Site I announcing the bingo game. Kids who lived in Site I housing also helped. Some worked the floor selling bingo cards and others worked a food stand selling soda pop, popcorn, hamburgers, and hot dogs. Teenage volunteers like Don Webster Jr. and his sisters worked the floor, selling cards and paying out winners in cash.

About fifty people, most of them Oneida, attended the first bingo session.

Cards were a dollar each for thirty games. Special games were twenty-five cents. The workers, mostly kids and moms, wore jeans and sweatshirts. Floorworkers kept bingo cards and money in canvas aprons with the words "Seymour Lumber Co." stenciled in big letters.

In the early days they didn't have round plastic chips to use as card markers. "So we opened sacks of dried commodity beans and corn from the kitchen and people used that to cover the squares," Sandy said.

The first bingo session was a modest success. Anabelle Skenandore won $115. The tribe took in $85. The proceeds from bingo and the sale of food were used to support the Oneida Nation Memorial Building, the *Kalihwisaks* reported.

The next week, September 26, Henry Skenandore and Ben Powless each won fifty dollars, while Mrs. Norb Hill and Dick Dodge each won twenty-five dollars. Jeff Metoxen, his brother, and his mother also won, according to the October 1, 1976, *Kalihwisaks*. The next bingo session would be held on October 3, the newsletter said. Just as one era was beginning, another was ending. October 3, 1976, was also the date that Irene Moore died at a Green Bay hospital after battling cancer. Her family had been caring for her at her home since her retirement.

Michelle (Powless) Hill told me she was turning ten when her grandmother Irene died. Even though Irene wasn't her biological grandmother—Michelle had been adopted by Lois and John Powless—the two were close. "I never realized that she never treated me any different than her very own granddaughter," Michelle said. "She taught me to sing 'Twinkle, Twinkle, Little Star,' driving down the road to Seymour in her big orange Buick. She loved pink; her comforter and bed pillows were pink. She always wore Mary Kay moisturizers that sat in a mirrored tray in pretty bottles on her dresser. She always had Chiclets in her glove compartment, dainty white handkerchiefs in her purse, and Luden's cough drops in her top dresser drawer. As 'tough' and hardworking as my grandmother was, my perception of her was very feminine."

"I didn't know she was dying," Michelle said. She went with Irene to Caroline Skenandore's house, where she saw some handmade Indian dolls, the kind that are cloth and stuffed. Michelle fell in love with one doll the minute she saw it. "I wanted her so badly and was sad because I couldn't get her. Grandma passed away October 3 and my birthday was October 10.

Grandma had gotten the doll for me and had arranged for my mom to give it to me on my birthday! That was my grandma."

Irene's niece, Madelyn Genskow, interviewed her about three months before she died.

"My aunt really was inspiring to me and many others," said Madelyn, who now lives in Waupaca.

Madelyn has been active in Oneida tribal affairs for most of her life. She is the daughter of Isaiah and Genevieve Cornelius, a niece of Sim Moore. Using a cassette tape recorder, Madelyn interviewed her aunt on July 5, 1976, in Irene's bedroom at her farm outside Seymour. Though she was in failing health, Irene's voice sounds clear and strong on the tape. Madelyn recalled that the windows were open on that summer day, and her Uncle Sim's tractor could be heard chugging past in the background.

She asked her aunt about her life, the progress the Oneida had made, and the direction of the tribe. "I think it's going both ways," Irene Moore said. "Some that's kind of negative, I think, but I don't blame the Indians much, especially the young people. Maybe they don't know which way to turn. Whereas older Indians know the values of their ancestors and we could teach the young ones that, but they don't always want to listen to us either. But I think it will come out all right. I think there's enough Indians thinking right and thinking for their own people that things will turn out, the way I see it."[8]

The Oneida tribal-run bingo game, which came to life at the same time Irene Moore's life was ending, was starting to forge bonds among players and community members alike.

Notes

1. Purcell Powless, Oneida Elder Interview with L. Gordon McLester III, Oneida Cultural Heritage Department, 2003.
2. L. Gordon McLester III and Laurence M. Hauptman, *A Nation within a Nation: Voices of the Oneidas in Wisconsin* (Madison: Wisconsin Historical Society Press, 2010).
3. Ernest Stevens Sr., the only son of Maria (Christjohn) Hinton, was born in Oneida in 1932 during the Depression and spoke only Oneida his first five years. Ernest was raised by Maria's grandmother after Maria

moved to Milwaukee to find work. Ernest graduated with academic and athletic achievements from Tigerton (Wisconsin) High School. He then joined the Marine Corps and served two combat tours in the Korean War. He returned to Oneida and married Marjorie Powless, and they had four children, Kelly, Ernest Jr., Coleman, and Toni. He attended the University of Wisconsin–Stevens Point and earned a bachelor's degree from Mt. Senario College. He worked for the Departments of Justice and the Interior in Washington, DC, in the Nixon administration. He was elected the first vice president of the National Congress of American Indians in 1973. He also was a Harvard MIT development fellow.

4. Ernest Stevens Sr. and Marjorie divorced in 1965. He returned to Oneida in 1976 with his new wife, Pat, who was from Pine Ridge, South Dakota. He and Pat had three children: David, Pamela, and Jennifer.

5. Megan Minoka Hill and Norbert Hill Jr., "Norbert Seabrook Hill Sr.," in *A Nation within a Nation: Voices of the Oneidas in Wisconsin*, edited by L. Gordon McLester III and Laurence M. Hauptman (Madison: Wisconsin Historical Society Press, 2010.

6. Ibid.

7. Purcell Powless, Oneida Elder Interview with L. Gordon McLester III, Oneida Cultural Heritage Department, 2003.

8. Irene Moore, interview with niece Madelyn Genskow, July 5, 1976, Seymour, WI.

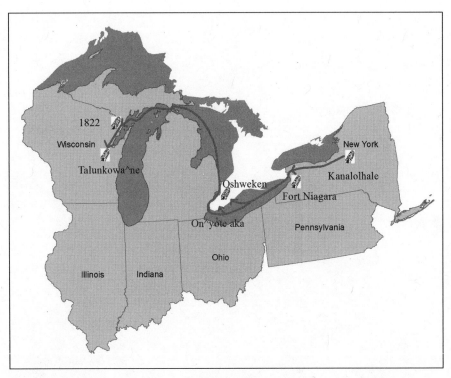

Several Indian nations, facing loss of homelands in New York state, emigrated west. The Oneidas moved by land and water routes through the Great Lakes and eventually resettled in the Fox River valley near Green Bay, Wisconsin. *Oneida Nation Geographic Land Information Systems Department*

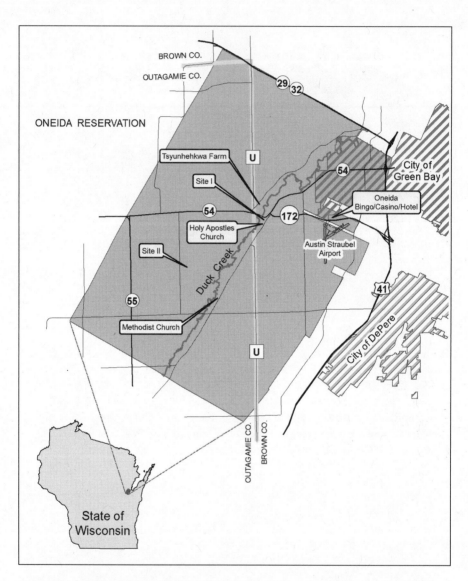

Original 1838 treaty boundaries of the 65,540-acre Oneida Indian Reservation, showing its location west of Green Bay and De Pere. *Oneida Nation Geographic Land Information Systems Department*

Paths of two families cross in the street of the old Salt Pork Avenue during Hoyan in 1962. Kids visit Oneida homes to collect doughnuts as part of the New Year's Day custom. *Press-Gazette Collection of the Neville Public Museum of Brown County*

Barbara John rests on a snowbank with her doughnuts during Hoyan in 1962 on old Salt Pork Avenue. *Press-Gazette Collection of the Neville Public Museum of Brown County*

This aerial photograph taken October 24, 1966, looking east, shows the beginning of construction of Site I housing. Duck Creek winds under the Highway 54 bridge at lower left. Holy Apostles Episcopal Church is at top right. The civic center would be built in the wooded area to the lower right seven years later. *Press-Gazette Collection of the Neville Public Museum of Brown County*

The newly elected Oneida Business Committee on August 9, 1967. Standing at left, Oscar Archiquette, vice chair, Purcell Powless, chair. Seated at left, Loretta Metoxen, secretary, and Joycelyn Ninham, treasurer. *Press-Gazette Collection of the Neville Public Museum of Brown County*

Top of the hill "downtown" Oneida photographed July 1968, looking east down Service Road from the railroad tracks. The area included Morgan's and Schroeder's markets, a tavern, and a laundromat. *Press-Gazette Collection of the Neville Public Museum of Brown County*

The Oneida Nation Memorial Building, better known as the civic center, was built in 1973 as a community activity center in the Site I housing development. Photo taken in 1974. *Kalihwisaks Collection, Oneida Tribe of Indians*

Irene Moore, known for recruiting and organizing others in tribal affairs and the first woman to chair the Oneida tribe, is shown November 28, 1975, at the time of her retirement. *Press-Gazette Collection of the Neville Public Museum of Brown County*

At right, David "Sonny" King, building and activity director at the civic center, plays foosball with staff member Tony Skenandore at the center in 1974. *Press-Gazette Collection of the Neville Public Museum of Brown County*

Rick Hill, standing at left, and Lieutenant Governor Martin Schreiber serve a Thanksgiving meal to Tony Stevens and Bobby Madrid on November 22, 1975, at the civic center. Rick Hill headed the Boys' Club at the time. In 1990, he succeeded Purcell Powless as chairman. In 1993, Rick became chairman of the National Indian Gaming Association. *Press-Gazette Collection of the Neville Public Museum of Brown County*

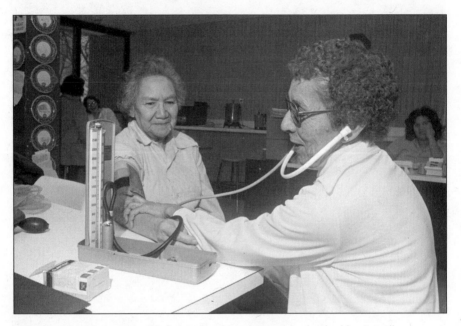

Oneida elder Mamie Ryan, left, has her blood pressure checked by Priscilla "Budgy" Manders, licensed practical nurse, at the civic center health clinic in January 1976. Priscilla Manders, Anna John, and Audrey Doxtator pushed for better health care for elders. The trio supervised Sunday night bingo in which profits supported the nursing home, later named for Anna John. *Press-Gazette Collection of the Neville Public Museum of Brown County*

CHAPTER 4

Extending the Rafters

I always thought the Indian way meant we
help each other for the common good. Unless
we all work together, everyone suffers.
—Oneida tribal chairman Purcell Powless,
September 29, 1978, *Kalihwisaks*

ALMA WEBSTER and Sandy Ninham grew up like many Oneida women of their era, yet with unique backgrounds. They came from families of different faiths, and though they had little money they managed to keep their kids fed and clothed. They shared what little they had with their neighbors in the Oneida community, including patched-up hand-me-down clothes.

Even though she spent much of her youth away from Wisconsin, Alma always thought of Oneida as her home. She was born in 1939 in Oneida as Alma Luedtke, daughter of Albert and Marie (Skenandore) Luedtke. She had a brother, Albert, and two sisters, Carol and Rugenne. The family lived on Service Road in Oneida and attended Holy Apostles Episcopal Church, known as the old stone church. Alma recalled walking the railroad tracks as a child up to her maternal grandparents' home off Riverdale Drive. The log home was between the railroad tracks and the road. It was the original homestead of Alma's grandparents, Nelson and Olive (Reed) Skenandore. Nelson was born October 5, 1882, to Jacob and Christine (Swamp) Skenandore. Nelson married Olive Reed, the daughter of John and Elizabeth (Cooper) Reed. One of their kids was Alma's mom, Marie.

"I remember they made cornbread the old way," Alma said of her grandparents. White corn was boiled with hardwood ashes to remove the hulls, then rinsed. The small bits from leftover corn soup also was used to make "slurp soup."

At age nine, Alma became an orphan. Her parents died of cancer just months apart. She and her siblings were sent to live at the Veterans of Foreign Wars National Home for Children in Eaton Rapids, Michigan. Her father had been a US veteran, and it was his wish that his kids be raised by the national home if anything happened to him, Alma said.

"It wasn't like an orphanage," she said. The siblings stayed together with a house mom in a single-family home on the campus. They attended public school in Eaton Rapids and went on shopping trips and to ballgames in Detroit.

The VFW National Home for Children was founded in 1925 as a step toward fulfilling its pledge to "honor the dead by helping the living." The home originated with an idea by a young Michigan woman named Amy Ross who wanted to help the families of World War I veterans. The home continues today to aid veterans and their families.[1]

At the home, Alma received Christmas gifts and birthday presents, simple luxuries some kids in Oneida didn't have. "It was a nice place. But I always knew I'd come back [to Oneida]," she said. She returned to Oneida in summers and stayed with her aunt and uncle, Emma and Robert Elmer. Emma was her dad's sister. They lived along Highway 54 near Duck Creek at what was called the Bow and Arrow Farm.

"It took me a month to get over leaving Oneida each summer. I'd cry all the way back. This was always home," Alma said.

As a young girl, she thought about becoming a gym teacher. After high school, at age eighteen, she enrolled in a college in Michigan but decided not to go and came back to Oneida. Her siblings stayed in Michigan. She lived with her aunt and uncle and got an office job working in billing and distribution at a Nabisco plant in Green Bay.

A friend later introduced her to a young Oneida man named Don Webster. They married in 1961 when she was twenty-two. "Don was Methodist. I grew up Episcopal," she told me. The family became regulars at the Oneida Methodist Church. Don worked in construction. Alma and Don moved into her maternal grandparents' log home, the one she remembered visiting as a child. She and Don were among the last inhabitants of the home. They later had three children, Melissa, Don, and Susan, and moved into a house a short distance away on West Service Road in Oneida. In the mid-1970s, when the kids were still young, the family bought a seven-acre farmstead a few miles south. Alma's friend, Sandy Ninham, was the one who told her about it.

"Sandy saw the home was for sale," Alma told me. "She liked it, but she already had a home of her own." It had space for a vegetable garden. Alma and her husband still live there today.

The log home of Alma's grandparents was typical of good craftsmanship. It was built solidly of squared-off, hand-hewn logs with interlocking joints at the ends. Cracks between logs were chinked with mortar. It is one of five such log homes preserved by the tribe as part of the Salt Pork Avenue project beginning in 1992. Logs from a sixth home were saved and used in reconstruction of the five homes. Tribal leaders felt that these older structures should be preserved as a part of Oneida's past. The handcrafted homes, three of them related to the same Skenandore family, are restored on the grounds of the Cultural Heritage Department near Highway 54 and Brown County FF.

"The homes are a direct link to our ancestors who began migrating from New York to Wisconsin in the early 1800s," tribal historian Loretta Metoxen said.

Alma and Sandy knew each other as young girls, and Sandy remembered hanging out with Alma when she was a teenager. "Alma had a car. We'd get a couple of dollars of gas and ride around Oneida and Seymour. We were single back then and would cruise around looking for boys," Sandy recalled. In high school, she never thought about a career other than becoming a mom and raising a family.

Sandy was born in 1943 in Oneida as Sandra Lee Doxtator, the first child of Leo and Betty (Bjerkvold) Doxtator. Her father, Leo Doxtator, was a descendant of Honyost Doxtator, who fought on the side of the Americans in the Revolutionary War. Honyost and his brother, Honyere Doxtator, had fought at the Battle of Oriskany. Many descendants of the brothers emigrated to Wisconsin in the early 1800s.[2] Loretta Metoxen told me that about three thousand Oneida people can trace their lineage to Honyere or Honyost Doxtator. Loretta herself is a descendant of Honyere Doxtator.

Betty and Leo raised fourteen children. Betty grew up Lutheran but converted to Catholicism, her husband's faith, when the couple married. All their kids were raised Catholic and attended St. Joseph's Church in Oneida, which was a short walk north from Salt Pork Avenue.

Until Sandy was four, the family lived in a house with a big picture window across from Schroeder's grocery store on West Service Road. "I remember the coffin of my baby sister sat in front of that window. I must have been three or four at the time," she said. Sandy's three-and-a-half-month-old sister, Patricia, had gotten sick about a week before Christmas and died of pneumonia. The family was unable to get her to a doctor in time; the nearest medical facility was ten miles away. The tiny coffin sat on an old round table with claw-foot legs. "I remember crawling under that table," Sandy said. The Oneida Hymn Singers came to the wake. "It was winter and we had a potbelly stove to keep warm. I remember the people who came by with food."[3] Sandy's parents bought two lots on Salt Pork Avenue for a homestead for their own growing family. The dirt road was said to have gotten its name from the smell of salt pork cooking in homes there. Salt pork came from pork belly, side pork, or fatback, the cheapest cuts and therefore most affordable. The town of Hobart renamed the road Shenandoah Drive in the 1960s. The tiny wood-frame house where Sandy's mom Betty lives today on Shenandoah Drive was moved to the site by tractor in the late 1940s. Betty recalled that Amos Christjohn sat atop the house with a pole to lift the electrical wires during the move. She said the house's front door was supposed to have faced south, not east, but the tractor broke down so the house remained oriented on that spot.

Betty and Leo later bought another two lots next door so they could have room for a vegetable garden. Betty grew corn, potatoes, cabbage, beans, and tomatoes, canning much of it. "If Mom hadn't frozen or dried or canned all that food, we would have starved," Sandy said. Betty made huge vats of sauerkraut and Leo bought fifty-pound bags of potatoes.

Leo Doxtator, nicknamed Chicken, was a laborer at Huron Cement and Leicht Dock and Warehouse in Green Bay. He also worked on railroad and construction crews. Some winters, he was laid off. The family had one car, which Betty drove on errands. Leo usually caught rides with coworkers into town.

Leo and Betty's other children, besides Sandra and Patricia, were Gloria, Everett, Nancy, Cleo, Carol, Gary, Michael, Allan, Jeff, Gerald, Dale, and

Michelle. The older kids slept above a cement-block garage. Sandy recalled waking up on cold mornings with frost on her blankets. Their home had no electricity until about 1953, when Sandy was ten. It had no plumbing or running water until about 1968, when Leo took out a loan for home improvements. The family had an outhouse in back and shared a well with neighbors.

"We used to get water from the hand pump up the hill," Betty said. They raised pigs and chickens. The boys raised rabbits. The pigs were known to break loose. "I just hated that. I went down the road banging on a pail with pig food trying to round them up," Betty said.

Neighbors kept an eye on everyone else's kids and often patched up winter coats to be reused by younger children. "Agnes Ness, Blanche McLester, Mrs. Tillie Baird, Johnny 'Git-Git' all watched out for us. You knew you were protected and watched out for, not just by your mom and dad," Sandy said. "Kids today don't have that."

In return, Betty and Leo often gave out baskets of groceries to help their neighbors in need. It seemed Betty was cooking meals for everyone from the time she got up until she went to bed.

One of Leo's sisters, Luella, lived on what was known as Stagger Lane, a dirt road on the east bank of Duck Creek just north of Highway 54. The cluster of a half dozen homes shared a common well. The homes were little more than tarpaper shacks. The lane may have gotten its name because of August Fern, who built some of the homes and ran a bar just staggering-distance away. Rosie Schuyler later took over the bar and added a small dancehall, which became quite a gathering spot. Sandy's wedding reception in 1962 was held at Rosie's. The bar eventually was torn down and Highway 54 was rerouted over the site where it stood. The homes on Stagger Lane were razed, and many residents moved into the Site I housing project in the late 1960s.

Betty's family often gathered for summer cookouts at Luella's. One meal featured chicken soup. It was made from the pet rooster belonging to Betty's eight-year-old son, Dale. "That rooster was mean. He'd attack if you hung up clothes," Betty said. "Dale wouldn't eat the soup."

In later years, Leo suffered from a degenerative disease and had to use a wheelchair. He died in 1989. One of Leo's brothers, Roman Doxtator, known as "Domey," served in World War II and later married Prudence Bennett, whom Sandy called Aunt Prudy. Aunt Prudy's mom, Lydia Bennett, as well as Sandy's paternal grandmother, Elizabeth Doxtator, spoke Oneida as their first language. They lived nearby and saw Sandy's family nearly every day. As a teen, Sandy babysat for Aunt Prudy's grandson while Prudy worked at Schroeder's Market. Domey died in 1971.[4]

"I lived with Aunt Prudy's family in high school," Sandy recalled. "I knew a few Oneida words just from listening to them. And I knew when they were talking about me because they'd say 'Sandra' in the middle of a conversation."

After high school, Sandy worked the summer in Milwaukee. On a trip home in about 1961, when Sandy was eighteen, she met a tall and handsome Oneida man named Leland "Lee" Ninham at St. Joseph's Catholic Church. Lee was a track star at Green Bay East High School and was hoping to run track in college. He was one of thirteen children of Nelson and Rebecca (Schuyler) Ninham, who lived along Duck Creek on Overland Road. As a child, Lee was sent to Tomah Indian School in Wisconsin.

Lee's maternal grandmother was Esther House, who married Sam Schuyler. After Sam died, Esther married Oscar Archiquette. Young people remember Esther and Oscar telling them the proper way to greet grandparents: *She ku a'khsot* (pronounced say-goo-ock-sote), meaning "Hello, Grandmother," and *She ku la'khsot* (pronounced say-goo-lock-sote), meaning "Hello, Grandfather."

Lee recalled that his father, Nelson, played violin and his mother, Rebecca, played piano. To help feed his family, Nelson speared fish and hunted deer, rabbit, and pheasant. "There were a lot of hardships growing up, but we always had something to eat," Lee said in a video interview with historian L. Gordon McLester III.

Lee and Sandy married in 1962. The families gathered at Rosie's tavern to celebrate the wedding.

"I was going to go to Northern Michigan [University] but I got married and started having kids," Lee said in the interview.[5] The couple named their first child Patricia, in memory of Sandy's little sister who had died in infancy. Three more kids followed about a year apart: Tim, Pamela, and Steve. The couple moved to Green Bay in the early 1960s and rented an apartment on Division Street on the city's near west side. Lee worked in the paper mills, first at Diana Manufacturing and then at Green Bay Packaging.

"The apartments were in Green Bay. There was no housing in Oneida back then," Sandy said.

Apartment life with four small kids and one income strained the family and the marriage. Lee and Sandy were on their own with no family nearby. Sandy took a job in housewares at the H. C. Prange store downtown. Prange's was a popular Green Bay landmark. Sandy brought her kids to Prange's Terrace Room restaurant overlooking the Fox River for "bunny plates." At Christmastime, crowds came to see Bruce the Spruce, the talking Christmas tree, and the store's elaborate window display. Yet Sandy felt cut off from her support network in Oneida. She was anxious whenever Lee was late getting home from the mill. One incident especially made her feel alone and vulnerable. "It was fall. I had taken a nutrition class at UW–Green Bay and forgot to pick up Pamela after kindergarten at Fort Howard Elementary School," Sandy said. "I rushed home to find her standing outside on our porch. She was OK. But to this day I have nightmares about it."

The couple returned to see family on the reservation whenever they could. Lee would bring his guitar and play Johnny Cash songs at family gatherings at Aunt Luella's. Their daughter, Patty, said she was about six or seven when her dad had her sing Tammy Wynette's song "Stand by Your Man" while he strummed.

Sandy credited faith and family with helping her during this difficult time. A key source of support was her sister-in-law Joycelyn, known as Joy, who was married to Lee's oldest brother, Vernon. Joy had served as Business Committee tribal treasurer from 1966 to 1969. At that time, the four committee offices included chair, vice chair, secretary, and treasurer. In 1969, the committee was expanded to nine, and Joy became one of five council members elected at large.

In about 1970, Joy suggested to Sandy that she and Lee move the family back to the reservation. By this time, the Site I housing development was well underway and had residences open for tribal members. She also told them to apply for a piece of undeveloped land that was to become available to tribal members. They got it. They had five years to build on the site on Florist Drive.

"I was really close to Joy. It was her way of getting us back home, back to our roots," Sandy said. "I had a lot of guardian angels, Joy and Vernon, Irene Moore, Ted Hawk's mom, Priscilla Manders."

Sandy and Lee lived in the Site I apartment for about a year. Lee continued to work in the paper mills near the Fox River, and the children switched
to West De Pere schools. The children's cousins, Joy and Vernon's sons,
Paul, Dan, and Mark, also went to West De Pere schools. Sandy and Lee's
duplex was at the corner of Artley and Doxtator Streets. The civic center,
meanwhile, was being built across the street. The Ninham family watched
that structure go up as Lee started to build the Florist Drive home with help
from his dad, Nelson, a trained bricklayer. The civic center and the family's
ranch house were finished in 1973, and the Ninhams moved into their own
house. Sandy and Lee's fifth child, Matthew, was born in 1975.

Sandy said the move back to the reservation helped renew their marriage and reconnected them to Oneida. Lee went hunting and fishing with
the kids, or pitched softballs to them in the backyard. Like many people,
Lee was a Green Bay Packers fan. He often parked players' cars at Lambeau Field on game days. He got tips and sometimes game tickets in return.
Lee had a football autographed by players of the late 1960s, and the family
tossed it around their yard until the names smeared.

Over the years, Lee stayed involved in athletics. He was a competitive
bowler, ranking seventh in the *Press-Gazette* individual bowling tournament in 1981. Like many young men in his community, he played recreation
league softball at the Oneida ballfields near Site I below Holy Apostles Episcopal Church. Back then, spectators would pull their vehicles up to the field
and sit on trunks and car hoods to watch. People held out dollar bills over
the fence to players who hit home runs or made big plays. Popular players
went home with dollars in their pockets, as well as women's phone numbers written on bar napkins.

Sandy began working with tribal programs, first helping Indian school
kids as part of the Johnson-O'Malley Act, then in the Community Action
Program and later as assistant director of the civic center. Lee worked nights
at the paper mill and watched Matthew in the mornings while Sandy was
at work. While her kids were still small, Sandy switched from St. Joseph's
Catholic Church and started attending Holy Apostles Episcopal Church.
She relied on her faith to get her through. "I'd be standing by the mailbox
by the side of the road. That's where I'd say my daily prayer. And then Alma
would come around and pick me up, and off to the civic center we'd go."

Bingo was just getting started at the civic center gym, she remembered.

"For each session we needed to staple together sheets of different colors and different control numbers. We didn't want to have multiple winners. We'd have lunch, then work until 2 p.m. Go home, get the Crock-Pot on, come back if it was bingo night. We brought our kids with us. I had five kids and Alma had three and Pat Misikin had one. We would have supper on and then we'd be off to bingo on Wednesday night and get done at around 10 p.m. We'd clean up really fast and get out of there. Then Lee went to work. My kids were all in sports, so Friday night there was no bingo because we went to basketball or football games with the kids at West De Pere High School."

Players bought one bingo entry card, or "hard card," for admission to the session and as many extra paper cards as they wanted, telling the cashier "one and five," or "one and six."

Many Oneida elders were return customers. One of the elders, Mamie Ryan, was known for her handcrafted black ash baskets. Mamie would always speak to the young workers in the Oneida language. When buying her bingo cards, she'd say *uskah* (pronounced uhs-gah) and *kaye*, (pronounced guy-yay)—the Oneida words for "one" and "four," according to Alma Webster's son Don, who attended West De Pere High School at the time and volunteered to work bingo. "The elders seemed disappointed when we couldn't talk to them in Oneida," he noted. There were only a few dozen native speakers left in the community.

In the beginning, bingo was a volunteer job aside from everyone's regular duties during the day. Stan Webster, an early volunteer at Oneida Bingo, told me that women of the tribe were the primary force behind the development of bingo. "I'm not saying men weren't involved, but if something needed to be done, women were the doers," Stan told me.

Sandy called on her siblings to help. Nancy, Jeff, Allan, and Dale were among those who worked bingo. Nancy volunteered in the early days and brought her children, Shannon, Aaron, and Annie, along to help. "They always needed volunteers. I went at first and handed out cards, then worked as a caller. The kids were too young to really work, so they picked up garbage," Nancy said.

Volunteers set up and took down tables and chairs each session in the gym. Jim Danforth, an Outagamie County sheriff's deputy, and Ted Hawk, a Brown County sheriff's deputy, were hired as security. Big Ronnie King also patrolled the grounds. Carl Prevost, Fritz Hill, and Allan Doxtator directed parking on the small streets and dirt lot in back. Nancy's husband, Greg Powless, worked as an Outagamie County sheriff's deputy. When he wasn't on duty, he'd help as a bingo caller. "My whole family was there anyway," Greg said.

Sandy's oldest daughter, Patty, said kids loved working bingo. "I think it was fun. We always had kids to work it. Mom was never short of kids. I think it gave us a purpose. We were pulling together. My brothers and sister and I worked it because Mom said we had to. Some of us would kind of grumble about being forced labor and would say, 'We don't want to be here but our moms are making us.' But other kids who weren't forced to be there came to hang out with their friends. And they came on their own. Plus when we provided service, the people in the community were always very appreciative. They praised the kids or gave us tips. That's why I think the kids liked it," Patty said.

Oneida Bingo gradually began to pay its workers: five or ten dollars a session for floorworkers and twenty dollars for callers. When the operation was sustainable to be able to pay people, Nancy Powless felt her time as a bingo worker was over. "Then we went on with our lives," Nancy said. Her husband, Greg, was needed as an additional security guard and stayed on for pay. Ted Hawk's sister, Cookie Kurowski, worked as a caller. When the gym began filling up to five hundred seats for bingo, security personnel were in demand. Jim, Ted, and Greg were later joined by Vern Doxtator, Ed King, Steve Hill, and Bill Sauer.

Michelle (Powless) Hill recalled going with her mom, Lois Powless, who played bingo a lot. "Sandy gave me my first job, I must have been twelve or thirteen," she said. "I cleaned up all the garbage after each session, clearing off the tables. I got five bucks a session. I loved it. Sometimes she would pay me more, like ten bucks. I would get my money at the end of the session. We would walk over to the bar that used to be across the road from Site I and I would get an Orange Crush and chips."

Sandy and the kids collected pop cans after all the bingo games. She loaded them up in an old green truck and took them in for recycling. With the money from selling scrapped pop cans, Sandy took the kids out for pizza.

Sandy's son, Steve Ninham, was eight or nine when he started his first job at bingo, picking up garbage and popcorn bags and sorting out soda cans. Sometimes he babysat his brother Matt. "Then I was promoted to bingo floorworker and I handed out cards. That was kind of fun, paying out bingo in cash. A lot of people from West De Pere schools worked bingo. Maybe twelve workers a shift or so. It would fill up the gym. I tried not to work Sunday night because I had school the next day. I came early to set up folding metal chairs and tables. I helped Mom with that stuff. We walked around with lumberjack aprons and handed out cards.

"I remember one time all these chairs were stacked up during a blackout game," Steve continued. "It was so quiet in there when calling numbers. I went and stood up against the bleachers. A couple hundred chairs were stacked up and I leaned against them and they all crashed down. I tried to pick them up and they fell down again."

"We pretty much ate lunch and dinner there," he added. "We always had a special on Sunday, chicken, chili, always a lot of popcorn. Our whole life centered around bingo at the time. Dad worked at Green Bay Packaging and Mom worked bingo." The family got two miniature shelties and named them Bingo and Tickets.

The family's schedule revolved around bingo, Sandy agreed. "We missed out on a lot of major holidays," she said. Bingo shut down for Good Friday, Easter, and Christmas, but other holidays were big days for bingo specials: New Year's, Memorial Day, Fourth of July, Labor Day, Thanksgiving. "So we ate our meal on Father's Day or Mother's Day, took the afternoon off, then worked bingo at night," Sandy said.

Steve recalled that it was smoky in the gym. "I always came home smelling of smoke. Your hair, clothes smelled," he said.

His sister, Pamela, remembered the smokiness, too. "We'd stand with the door open in back so we had fresh air circulating," she said. "In winter we couldn't do it, because the old people wouldn't let us open it and let in cold air. Even our socks reeked of smoke. But I learned customer service and how to be nice to people. Mom and Alma were strict. They told us to be nice to them even if you don't like them, and how to be punctual."

Patty said the amount of their pay depended on the success of the game. "Maybe that was part of the excitement. You worked hard and sold more cards and we'd get more in cash at the end if the game earned more money. I remember going to high school and trying to recruit volunteers who weren't Oneida. Maybe they played on the basketball team with me and were looking for clothes money. They wanted to work."

Patty said bingo supervisor Lillian King usually came to her bingo shift straight from her full-time job in the planning office of Moore Business Forms (now part of RR Donnelley). After bingo, Lillian returned to her other full-time job, running a home as a mother. "I enjoyed bingo," Lillian told me. "I loved doing it and enjoyed helping the tribe."

Lillian's comment hinted at something several women told me: that working bingo didn't seem like work. Their power came from communal effort, pooling their skills and sharing the load.

I have a story of my own that demonstrates this. When our daughters were young, my wife, Patty, would stay up late to finish making their pow-wow outfits in time for the next day's grand entry. Working alone, she became tired and irritable. One year, Patty's sister Pamela and a friend came over to work on their powwow outfits. They chatted and laughed as they worked at the dining room table. One who was better at sewing took charge of that while another who was better at beading helped the other two. They brainstormed new designs and ideas. By morning, the women had accomplished more together than the sum of what they could have separately. Her mom, Sandy, said it was like that with bingo. "It was always happy work. People were having fun. There was camaraderie. We were constantly looking for ways to make the games more exciting or get the people through the line faster," she said.

Alma said the key to bingo's success was getting patrons to buy in. "We used whatever we took in for our prize," Alma said. With bigger crowds, they could offer bigger jackpots. "We didn't have any idea how to run bingo at first," she said. They based it on the way bingo was played at churches and veterans charities.

"We introduced all kinds of varieties," Sandy said. "Large and small picture frame, T, diagonal. We came up with specials: Jumbo Oneida, Three Sisters, Oneida Downs, Diamond, or X. For a big jackpot, you'd get the big pot if it went in twenty-five numbers or less. Every night we would add money to that pot. The more we added to it, the more people came in, and so it grew and grew."

Alma Webster came up with many ideas for bingo, such as marathon bingo and early bird bingo. She was usually on the sidelines, tallying up the receipts. One night she called Sandy over and told her, "We have this much money. Let's raise the jackpot to seven hundred dollars." That was two hundred dollars above what had been advertised. Sandy got on the microphone to make the announcement. The unexpected jackpot added to the game's spontaneity and excitement.

Some players used their household money to pay for gambling. "I remember feeling bad when a lady came through the line and said this was her rent money and that she hoped to double it. I feel a little guilty about that," Sandy said. Nevertheless, the benefits of bingo seemed to outweigh the negatives. On the whole, most people gambled responsibly, Sandy said.

Sunday afternoon sessions filled up quickly, so after a few months organizers added bingo on Wednesday evenings at the civic center. "That was a school night, so kids weren't using the gym," Sandy said. Later, two more sessions were added, on Saturday and Sunday evenings. The profits from Sunday evening bingo sessions were earmarked for the nursing home.

Audrey Doxtator, Anna John, and Priscilla Manders worked the Sunday night bingo session, selling food or cigarettes. "A lot of people were involved in making money for the tribe," Amelia Cornelius said.

Pretty soon, bingo was scheduled four days a week. That was good for bingo, but it added a challenge, as the gym was also used for sports, concerts, Friday night socials, dances, and roller skating. "I remember we'd have to take down volleyball nets and fill the floor with tables and chairs," Patty said. "Maybe a tournament would barely end in time for us to get in there and set up. It was a very active place. Then we had GTC [General Tribal Council] meetings there for a while. We got a lot of use out of that gym. I think bingo allowed tribal members from all parts of the reservation to come to one place and do something together. So it helped build relationships with each other." The Oneida reservation was divided among five school districts, and after class, kids usually went off in different directions. "There weren't many opportunities to meet kids from the west or south side of the reservation unless they were relatives. So it allowed us to interact and become friends," she said.

In the summer of 1977, a few Oneida Bingo games were held in the Sacred Heart Center cafeteria, the *Kalihwisaks* reported. Profits from those games helped provide food to the needy in the area. Called Top of the Hill Bingo, these games were smoke-free. "Thanks to many volunteers who helped make the three bingo games at the seminary a big success for the emergency food pantry. Despite hot conditions everyone worked hard and the turnout was tremendous," wrote Carol Nicholas in the July 22, 1977, *Kalihwisaks*.

Otherwise, the Oneida Bingo games were always in the civic center gym. It was a most unlikely spot for a commercial enterprise: the gym was in the middle of a low-income tribal housing project. Some non-Indian players were scared to drive into the HUD housing project at first. And some Oneida families were afraid of the hundreds of cars now entering the small neighborhood where children played. Both sides had some uneasiness to overcome.

Debbie Skenandore was fifteen when she and her sister, Brenda, began working the kitchen during bingo sessions in 1976. She said Sandy Ninham's friendly manner helped ease players' fears about entering an Indian reservation and likewise calmed Oneida residents worried about strangers and traffic coming into a neighborhood where kids played. Sandy made everyone feel welcome. "Sandy knew people were coming there for entertainment. So she made it fun," Debbie said.

Cash wasn't the only incentive for players. Workers handed out colored eggs at Easter, roses on Mother's Day, and prizes for best Halloween costumes among players and workers. Sandy recalled that she, Alma, and Pat Misikin drove to Brussels in Door County each fall to pick apples to be given away at bingo sessions.

One snowy night after a bingo session that probably should have been canceled due to bad weather, Alma was driving Sandy home when her 1974 Plymouth Duster skidded off Florist Drive at a curve in the road and got stuck in a snowbank. "We just laughed," Sandy recalled. "We were probably giggling before; maybe that's why it happened." They left the car where it was and were picked up by Lee Ninham, who was following with their kids in a second car. Alma's son Donny and husband, Don, came the next morning to pull the car out.

People in Green Bay and De Pere heard about Oneida Bingo either by word of mouth or from handmade signs or flyers. The crowds quickly grew to several hundred people. One of the attendees was Linda Lodel, a young woman who lived in Sheboygan at the time. "I started coming with two or three girlfriends as a day out," she told me in a phone interview from her home in Chilton, Wisconsin. "It was like church bingo, but more exciting. The payouts were bigger. I would win a jackpot once in a while, fifty or a hundred dollars. I always thought someday I'd win the big one." Like many players, she followed rituals: sitting in the same area and setting out little troll dolls, good-luck charms, on her table next to her pack of cigarettes. "You had to get there early. So we played cards—sheepshead—while we waited."

Regular players like Linda knew not to discount the role of luck. But being alert can be more important than being lucky. Serious players knew they had to concentrate when playing a half-dozen cards at once. "Sleepers," the name for players who miss numbers because they aren't paying attention, account for many lost jackpots. If they don't yell "Bingo!" before the next ball is called, they're out of luck. The regulars knew some tricks: bring a seat cushion to stay comfortable, coffee to keep alert, snacks to keep up your energy.

Making sure players were comfortable and happy was a main goal of managers. None of the bingo managers had a college education, but they all had strong leadership skills, Patty told me. "They worked hard to make it fun. They didn't take no for an answer. It didn't happen on its own," she said. Supervisors made sure the kitchen and bathrooms were kept clean and the food was good. They were particular even about what kind of hot dog and hamburger they served. The managers tried to use local businesses and suppliers they knew. On Valentine's Day or Mother's Day, managers held a drawing for a box of Seroogy's chocolates, a longtime candy maker in De Pere. "I think that was all part of their strategy to make it a community effort and make sure everybody benefited," Patty said.

Another early player who became a regular was Shirley Czech of Green Bay. Several Oneida people remember her as the friendly redhead who's been coming to bingo for decades. Shirley recalled that early games at the civic center gym were run quite informally—by mostly high school kids and young moms dressed casually. Pat Misikin or Audrey Doxtator would collect money at the door, using a wooden box as a cash register, she said.

For some non-Indian bingo players like Shirley, it was the first time they'd set foot on a reservation. "Bingo was a kind of icebreaker, a way to get to know our neighbors," said Shirley, who came with her husband, Al, from their home on Green Bay's west side to play bingo. Their home off Highway 54 was at one time in the town of Hobart and later annexed into the city of Green Bay.

Shirley, the mother of three boys, said she started playing bingo at Oneida after her mother died. "It was a stress reliever," she said. "Before bingo I had lived in this area for many years and really had no way to mingle and get to know Oneida people." From her house she often saw Oneida driving by or walking past. "But we really got to know them better after their bingo games began. We met so many nice people there."

Shirley, a substitute schoolteacher now in her seventies, still plays Oneida bingo. For our interview, Shirley brought along a notepad filled with more than a hundred names of bingo workers, players, and young people she'd met over the years because of bingo. Based on her contacts from bingo, Shirley joined the Oneida Dodo Club, the social club for grandparents, and is one of the few non-Indians in the club. For Shirley, the attraction to bingo was mostly social. The chance to meet people was more important than the chance to win money.

The bingo ladies in the late 1970s started offering games and activities that stimulated social interaction. Shirley said one such game was "buddy bingo," in which players sitting next to a winner shared in the spoils and each won two dollars. It made the game more social, since you could cheer on your neighbor if you didn't win, she said.

Stan Webster, an early bingo volunteer, said it's hard to know what made Oneida Bingo so appealing. But from the beginning, it was more than just the chance to win big jackpots or beadwork prizes, he said. "In the first few months of bingo, we had no microphone. The caller was placed on a platform about three feet high," Stan said. That way, the players could hear numbers called and the caller could see when people signaled they had won.

The caller, with one hand, turned a small wire cage that contained seventy-five numbered wooden balls until one ball rolled into a pocket and out into the caller's other hand. Sometimes the wooden ball would fall out and hit the floor and the caller would chase the ball as it bounced across the gym floor.

"One time Alma asked me, 'Can you call?' I said, 'Sure,'" Stan said. Alma told him to make sure he made announcements in between calling numbers. Stan said floorworkers and bingo ladies handed him notes of people's birthdays, anniversaries, engagements, marriages, and new babies. "We'd announce rummage sales, families who had a rough time, house fires, kids killed in car wrecks, families who needed support or some kind of help," Stan told me. "It was family entertainment. Perhaps it was because no alcohol was allowed on tribal property. It was not bingo so much as a community gathering."

Two other regulars who became like family members at Oneida Bingo were Harold "Whitey" Klika and his wife, Audrey. Whitey was the long-time manager of the Bay Theater in downtown Green Bay.

Born in 1915 in Green Bay, Whitey met Audrey in the second grade. He graduated from Green Bay East High School and began working at the Bay Theater in 1934 as a doorman. He was later promoted to cashier and eventually manager. He served in the army in World War II, then returned to manage the Bay Theater until he died at age sixty-six. When he started at the Bay, theaters were a Depression-era escape. At that time, the theater combined movie showings with vaudeville shows. Louis Armstrong played there. A Wurlitzer pipe organ played for community sing-alongs before each show.

The ornate theater at 117 South Washington Street opened in 1930 as the Fox Theatre and was renamed the Bay in 1933. It was designed to look like a Moorish-influenced Spanish courtyard with stars twinkling in the midnight-blue ceiling. Those were "the lush years" for the Bay, Whitey told an interviewer a few years before his death.[6]

But downtowns across the country were struggling in the 1970s and many old movie palaces were torn down or converted to multiplexes. Several downtown Green Bay landmarks, like Kaap's Restaurant, were demolished as part of an urban renewal project that created Port Plaza retail mall. In 1978, the Bay Theater was remodeled into three cinemas as a way to stay competitive. Partitions painted black separated two screens in the lower level. Dropped ceilings covered up the lavish courtyard architecture in the balcony screen. The Bay closed as a movie theater in 1993.

A community fund-raising effort in 1999 was launched to restore the the-ater's original architecture, and it reopened in 2002 as the Meyer Theater. Whitey Klika didn't live to see the restoration. "I don't think he liked the change to a triplex, but he probably didn't have much say in it," said Judy Sustman of Green Bay, one of two daughters of Harold and Audrey Klika.

The Klikas were fixtures at bingo games at the civic center until Whitey's death on November 2, 1981. They were returning from an Oneida bingo game when Whitey suffered a massive heart attack. Whitey never drove; Audrey did all the driving. The family lived within walking distance of downtown their whole lives, Judy said.

"My dad knew everybody. He knew Packers players. He met Nat King Cole. He was well liked," Judy told me. "My parents went to bingo all the time." Once they were judges for a Halloween costume contest at bingo.

Whitey and Audrey enjoyed getting to know all the bingo workers. Lisa (Hill) Behringer, a teenage bingo worker in the late 1970s, said Whitey often let Oneida bingo workers in for free when he recognized them at the Bay Theater. Sandy Ninham could attest to that. She said that one time at the Bay Theater, Whitey saw her and her family in line for a movie and wouldn't let them pay. "He found Lee and gave him his money back," Sandy said. "He was always willing to help us."

Whitey also gave the bingo ladies advice about running their concession stand. At Whitey's suggestion, the bingo hall switched from canned soda to fountain soda using carbonated tanks.

"Whitey Klika gave them advice how to sell soda and how to price it. That's an example of how they worked with local community businesses," Patty said.

Judy Sustman said when the Green Bay Packers were playing on Sun-days, her father would listen to the games on a transistor radio at the same time he tracked his bingo cards. "How he did both, I don't know," she said.

Many people were fans of bingo and football. The bingo hall had no TV, but a caller often would announce score updates. Patty was calling bingo one Sunday during a close game between the Packers and their archrival Chicago Bears. "The Bears won!" she told the crowd during a break in the action, the announcement drawing a chorus of boos. "I'm just kidding. The Packers won!" she answered with a laugh. The crowd responded with even louder boos and handfuls of popcorn for having been teased.

Football is not taken lightly in a community whose identity is so strongly tied to the Packers. The early years of Oneida Bingo coincided with disappointing seasons for the Pack. Under head coach Bart Starr, the team was 4–10 in 1975, 5–9 in 1976, 4–10 in 1977, 8–7–1 in 1978, 5–11 in 1979, and 5–10–1 in 1980. The team improved under Starr to 8–8 in 1981, 5–3–1 during the strike-shortened 1982 season, and 8–8 in 1983.

Packers fans and the team had managed to hang on through lean years and troubled eras before. Football had been a popular spectator sport in Green Bay since the 1890s, with new town teams forming each season. Several Oneida men played on those town teams, having learned the game of football at Indian boarding schools. One of the top players on Green Bay's 1897 championship team was Tom Skenandore of Oneida, who had learned to play at Carlisle. He was the first and only paid player, if there was any money to pay him.[7]

The Packers were founded in the old Cherry Street offices of the *Green Bay Press-Gazette* on August 11, 1919, by Curly Lambeau, a former Notre Dame player from Green Bay, and George Calhoun, sports editor of the *Green Bay Press-Gazette*. Lambeau worked as a shipping clerk at the Indian Packing Company, a wartime meat-processing plant, and talked his employer into paying for team jerseys. The company folded in a year, but the team name stuck. Those were the days of passing the hat to pay expenses. As costs of team franchises escalated, the community pitched in to keep the team afloat. A. B. Turnbull, general manager of the *Press-Gazette,* lobbied a group of local businessmen known as the Hungry Five and formed the Green Bay Football Corporation. It became the National Football League's only publicly owned corporation. Under Lambeau's leadership, the Packers won championship titles six times: 1929, 1930, 1931, 1936, 1939, and 1944.[8]

The corporation sold stock to keep the team competitive with bigger cities. Bond sales financed the building of a new home stadium in 1956, the same year quarterback Bart Starr was drafted by the Packers in the seventeenth round. The team's Green Bay home field had been the East High School football field, known as the old city stadium. The new city stadium at the southwest edge of town was dedicated in 1957 and renamed Lambeau Field in 1965. In Starr's first five seasons, his interceptions were nearly double his touchdowns. That changed with the 1959 arrival of head coach Vince Lombardi, who recognized Starr's potential. With Starr as quarterback, the team won league championships in 1961, 1962, 1965, 1966, and 1967. The last two titles were Super Bowls I and II, for which Starr was named Most Valuable Player. After he retired from playing in 1971, Starr became quarterbacks coach for the Packers in 1972. He was head coach from 1975 to 1983.

With that football heritage, Packers fans like Whitey Klika managed to survive the lean years on the hope that success was around the corner. Professional football managed to survive in small-town Green Bay because the community got behind the team. Oneida Bingo managed to thrive in large part because of community support, both tribal and nontribal. Oneida Bingo managers, too, were beginning to hope—after decades of deteriorating economic conditions on the reservation—that they finally might have a success to build on. For Oneida, survival as a tribe was at stake.

The Oneida tribe employed just fifteen people in 1970. By September 1978, it employed one hundred people. By 1980, the tribe would have 350 employees. "I always thought the Indian way meant we help each other for the common good," chairman Purcell Powless said in the September 29, 1978, issue of the *Kalihwisaks*. "Unless we all work together, everyone suffers."

By the late 1970s, bingo was bubbling with fans and foes inside and outside of Oneida. There were growing conflicts over bingo, tobacco, and the civic center. Into this growing chaos, leaders stepped up.

Notes

1. The VFW National Home for Children, www.vfwnationalhome.org.
2. Genealogical record of Sandra (Doxtator) Ninham, Oneida Cultural Heritage Department.
3. Sandra (Doxtator) Ninham, Oneida Elder Interview with L. Gordon McLester III, Oneida Cultural Heritage Department, 2004.
4. Prudence Doxtator also was a longtime member of the Oneida Hymn Singers. Her brother was Robert Bennett, who served as US Commissioner of Indian Affairs 1966–1969. She also worked for years as a librarian at the Oneida Library. She died at age ninety-three in 2009.
5. Leland Ninham, Oneida Elder Interview with L. Gordon McLester III, Oneida Cultural Heritage Department, 2004.

6. "Bay Theater Manager Dies," *Green Bay Press-Gazette*, November 2, 1981.
7. Denis J. Gullickson and Carl Hanson, *Before They Were Packers: Green Bay's Town Team Days* (Black Earth, WI: Trails Books, 2004).
8. "Birth of a Team and a Legend," Green Bay Packers website, www. packers.com.

CHAPTER 5

The Bingo Queens

By EARLY 1977, bingo sessions were being held at the civic center gym on Wednesday nights, Saturday nights, and Sunday afternoons and evenings. It was becoming a full-time job for Alma Webster and Sandy Ninham.

"Pretty soon it got to be so much work. After every game, I still had to be [Business Committee] treasurer," Alma said. "It was too much fun. I like bingo, playing it and running it." She soon realized she couldn't run bingo and be treasurer while also taking care of three teens and a husband. Instead, she resigned as tribal treasurer and focused on running Oneida Bingo, according to the March 21, 1977, Business Committee minutes.

Sandy opted to remain with Oneida Bingo, too, resigning as civic center assistant director nearly three months later, effective June 17, 1977. The *Kalihwisaks* offered her "a special thanks for all the time and effort given to the community."

Tribal leaders began to take notice of the bingo profits within the first year of operation. Ada Deer, a Menominee leader active in many native issues nationwide, recalled meeting with Oneida tribal leaders during the 1970s. "I remember when bingo started at the civic center," Ada told me. "I was at a meeting with vice chairman Norbert Hill Sr. and he said simply, 'It's making money!' He was kind of surprised and amazed and full of pride all at once," Ada said.[1]

Stan Webster, who volunteered at Oneida Bingo, said there had been the perception that any Oneida business venture would fail if it was on the reservation and the Oneida were running it. But bingo was overcoming pessimistic attitudes. This Oneida-run venture was different. For once, a business running on "Oneida power" was succeeding, he said.

Sandy and Alma told me they know why Oneida Bingo was successful: because it was run by women. "It was, really," Alma said.

"From the beginning, women always ran it," Sandy continued. "I think it was successful because we weren't greedy. We did it for one reason: to pay the bills. We did it to take care of our people and our kids."

While tribal officials were aware of the bingo profits being made at the civic center gym, not everyone in Oneida was happy with bingo. Some people felt gambling wasn't a proper business for a tribe. Some felt encouraging non-Indians to come to the reservation would hurt tribal culture. Youths were disappointed to find the gym often closed to them and open instead to cigarette-smoking bingo players. People started complaining to tribal chairman Purcell Powless or members of the Business Committee.

A story in the November 11, 1977, *Kalihwisaks* focused on the growing conflict over use of the civic center. "There is a question of the importance to make money in use of the building or to allow sports and every other activity to take place," the story said. What was the real reason the building was bought? Sonny King, the building director, was responsible for maintenance and balancing community use. "Contact Sonny and give him your opinions. Talk to the program people before you complain to the Business Committee," the story said.

Ernest "Ernie" Stevens Jr., a self-described roughneck teenager who had been booted out of several schools for fighting, was the kind of youth the civic center was designed to help and Sonny King was trying to steer. He was big for his age and rebellious, and he wore his hair in a long braided ponytail. He had a temper and wouldn't back down from a fight with anyone, including basketball referees. At age sixteen, Ernie was a promising heavyweight boxing champ and an underage tavern brawler. At seventeen, he stood an imposing six-foot-four and was an avid basketball player. Folks in Oneida thought he was capable of doing big things, though they weren't sure if they would be bad things or good things.

His father, Ernest Stevens Sr., was a policy maker in Washington and was well respected for his work on behalf of Indian nations. Ernest Sr. was credited with helping resolve the BIA takeover by Indian activists in 1972. He was elected the first vice president of the National Congress of American Indians in 1973. He also headed the American Indian Policy Review Commission in Washington, DC, in 1975.

But a father was missing in young Ernie's life. His dad and mom, Marjorie (Powless) Stevens, had divorced when Ernie was five and the family was living in Los Angeles. His older brother, Kelly, was six, brother Coleman was four, and sister Toni was two. Ernie and his three siblings lived with their mom in the tough sections of Los Angeles and Milwaukee before moving back to Oneida in 1974, when Ernie was fifteen. Ernie saw his father around the community after Ernest Sr. moved to Oneida in 1976 with his second family: his new wife, Pat, who was from Pine Ridge, South Dakota, and their three children, David, Pamela, and Jennifer.

As a teen, Ernie had been acting as if he were on his own as an adult: joining AIM protests, carrying a gun at Wounded Knee, volunteering at Indian centers, and working at his uncle's pool hall. Returning to the small reservation was a culture shock, he told me. His mom, Marjorie, who was active in AIM, was often away on marches and protests. As a result Ernie had little direct parental supervision.

"I was used to being on my own," he said. That changed when his family moved back to Oneida. Returning to Oneida where people knew him forced him to slow down and be a kid again. He lived for a time with his grandmother, Maria (Christjohn) Hinton, and his aunt, Lorraine (Powless) Cornelius. They made sure he went to bed at a regular time and got up for school. He had his mom's car (back problems made it hard for her to drive) but no driver's license. He got away with driving in Milwaukee, but not in Oneida. Local Oneida deputies like Ted Hawk and Greg Powless knew he had no license and would be watching if he were cruising the rez.

"Like my dad, I wanted to be a leader. Because of the divorce, he wasn't there. There was a void in my life," he told me. He looked to other men as father figures, and many women elders helped him. Eva Danforth, a Job Service counselor, got him into a GED (General Educational Development) program.[2] Sonny King encouraged him to play basketball, and boxing coach Lou Askenette trained him for Golden Gloves competition. As a result, he spent a lot of time at the civic center. He also was one of the Oneida youths who resented sharing the gym with bingo players.

"The civic center was my life back then. It was where I lived, worked, and played basketball," Ernie told me. "That's what I wanted to do: play Indian ball. I was six-foot-four and had an attitude. Sonny King would scrounge up baseballs, bats, and shoes for us. They tried to come up with the money to pay for the equipment with raffles and fund-raisers. Bingo was starting at the civic center then. The workers set up tables and chairs on the gym floor for bingo sessions. I didn't let it stop me. I'd go in there and clear the chairs away from a circle so I could shoot baskets. That would piss off the bingo managers, because I wouldn't put the chairs back when I was done," he said.

Sandy Ninham tried to keep Ernie in line. "She'd tell me to put the chairs back. But I had a chip on my shoulder. I couldn't understand why we couldn't play. One time I got into an argument with her in the hallway. The word got back to Uncle Purcell and Sonny King for them to talk to me. I wanted them to believe I could be a leader. But I had a temper," he said.

Sandy recalled the hallway confrontation, too. Ernie, towering a foot over Sandy, argued that the civic center's gym had been built for Oneida kids, not bingo players. Sandy countered that revenue from bingo was helping Oneida youths in the long run. "We need those bingo players to pay the bills so you can play," Sandy recalled telling him.

"Sandy took me over her knee a few times," he said, referring to the verbal spanking.

Ernie often uses figures of speech like that. He didn't mean she was treating him like a child but that she was trying to get him to see the bigger picture. Sometimes the collective needs outweigh the personal wants. The boys wanted to shoot baskets, but the women needed to put food on the table. Operating bingo in the gym would mean sacrifices and changes in the way people lived.

Ernie said Alma Webster helped him understand by breaking it down into simple math for him. It takes twenty minutes for the gym's fluorescent lights to warm up once they're turned off, Ernie recalled Alma telling him. "Without money from bingo, we'll have to leave the lights off and close the building," she explained.

"I had no idea what bingo or gaming was about back then. But in a cock-eyed way, I understood what having those lights on meant. Alma took the time to make me understand. Alma and Sandy, they tag-teamed on me." Ernie gave credit to his elders for trying to straighten him out. But it wasn't easy, and it took him years to control his temper. In the fall of 1978, Ernie was hired as recreation director at the civic center. He lost that job during cutbacks in 1980, then was passed over for the job when it was reposted. People were concerned that some of his behavioral habits made him a poor role model for youths, he said.

"Some people in Oneida were betting on me to fail," he told me. Ernie left Oneida in fall 1981 for Haskell Indian Junior College in Lawrence, Kansas, as a walk-on to the basketball team. "The Haskell world is where I learned about responsibility," he said.

With help from many corners, Ernie eventually returned to Oneida as a husband and father to a young family. He and his wife, Cheryl, have seen all of their five kids enter college. He recalled how the bingo ladies in the 1970s were trying to help the kids of the community.

"I don't think these women cared about sovereignty. They just wanted to turn the lights on for us. They knew how many kids were walking out on the highway out here. Recreation took the place of night life, the wrong life. These ladies wanted kids to hang out in places where they could be safe and they could learn. I was just one of those kids running around," Ernie said.

When bingo started, most people thought it would earn pin money to help pay bills. Tribal chairman Purcell Powless and the Business Committee agreed to put 10 percent of the profits away each week for a building fund. "Alma said, 'Can we put 10 percent away for a new building?' I said sure, go ahead," Purcell recalled in an interview in 2003. "I didn't realize how much they were making at bingo."[3]

Alma and other managers realized early on that bingo needed a building of its own if it was to succeed.

Oneida Bingo generated $2,165 in the final quarter of 1976. In its first full year of operation, 1977, the game generated $46,421 for the tribe, according to Bingo Committee records. That paid the center's light bill with a lot left over. The next year would bring in three times that.

Purcell Powless was later asked to guess the size of the building fund. He expected it to be around three thousand or four thousand dollars. To his surprise, it was more than ten times that amount. The tribal gaming operation, the first in Wisconsin, was becoming one of the most successful such operations in the country.[4]

As bingo revenue grew, so did organization and structure. What would be done with the surplus profits? Would other Oneida programs be funded?

The November 25, 1977, issue of *Kalihwisaks* carried a story on the topic. According to the story, the Business Committee suggested that Sonny King present a plan at a future meeting for saving a portion of bingo funds. Programs that sought bingo funds would present a request to the Business Committee under guidelines of the tribe's bingo ordinance. Any complaints in regard to the center would be submitted in writing to the chairman.

As 1977 wound to a close, the Oneida tribe was seeing many efforts come to fruition. A grand opening was set for October 14–15 for the new Oneida nursing home. The first residents were admitted to the nursing home January 3 of the following year. The Oneida Health Center adjoining the nursing home was 60 percent complete and would accept its first patients over the winter of 1977–1978, the *Kalihwisaks* reported.

The Business Committee, on February 6, 1978, discussed making improvements to the civic center to accommodate bingo players, including air conditioning for the gym, additional storage area, and a bigger parking lot. At the February 20 committee meeting, Norbert Hill moved to have 20 percent of all gross proceeds from bingo held in escrow until they could be entered into the general fund.

An editorial in the March 3, 1978, *Kalihwisaks* reflected a new attitude toward reservation life. "There has been a kind of Indian renaissance—a renewal of pride in the old ways," it said. Reservations have now proved to be "enclaves of cultural preservation." The editorial did not specifically mention bingo but said, "Tribes have begun to build an economic base in ways which to them are seen as culturally, economically and environmentally sound."

At the March 20 Business Committee meeting, Norbert Hill moved to approve creation of a Bingo Committee that would oversee the operation. A five-member committee was approved, consisting of Audrey Doxtator, Alma Webster, Pat Misikin, Sandy Ninham, and Sonny King. Each Bingo Committee member, except Sonny, was expected to supervise a bingo session each week. Business Committee member Loretta Metoxen moved to earmark bingo proceeds on two Sunday evenings a month for the nursing home and for youth and recreation.

Tribal groups began making funding requests directly to the Bingo Committee, which in turn made recommendations to the Oneida Business Committee. Minutes of Business Committee meetings that spring indicate that bingo proceeds were used to help pay expenses for the new nursing home, for industrial development, and to cover a thousand-dollar deficit in the general fund.[5] The Bingo Committee also realized the civic center wouldn't be able to accommodate both bingo players and youth recreation over the long term. They needed a new building. Bingo was being held in the gym four times a week, and people were often turned away. The gym held 450 comfortably but sometimes squeezed in more than 500 players. The potential for bingo's success was limited only by the size of the building.

At a special Business Committee meeting held November 30, 1978, the Bingo Committee discussed with tribal leadership the possibility of expanding bingo and building a new structure outside Site I. A new building would cost about $350,000 and could include a kitchen, parking, and room to accommodate eight hundred people. The Business Committee approved placing bingo profits not already allocated to another purpose into a special interest-bearing bank account.

Oneida's profits came at the expense of other bingo charities in the Green Bay area, however. Mary Mullin, a parishioner who helped start a bingo fund-raiser at Ashwaubenon's Nativity of Our Lord Catholic Church in 1970, recalled that her church's bingo crowd "was cut in half" after Oneida Bingo expanded its operation in the late 1970s. "It hurt us but I never begrudged the Oneidas their success," she told me. Mary was born and raised in Escanaba, in Michigan's Upper Peninsula, about an hour north of Green Bay and grew up playing bingo in Gladstone, Michigan, with her mother. Growing up near other tribes, she also was aware of the hardships Indians faced. Mary later became a bingo inspector for the state and checked on games throughout northeastern Wisconsin, although her inspections did not include Indian bingo halls. "Oneidas were always the underdogs. I knew they were honest people. I say more power to them," Mary told me.[6]

Not all Catholic bingo organizers were as magnanimous. "We knew they were upset because their players would come to our bingo games and tell us," Sandy said.

Oneida Bingo stirred complaints from higher sources, too. One of them was a Catholic priest, Father Robert Cornell, who served double duty as a US congressman at that time.[7] "I remember that congressman, that Father Cornell, called me and asked us to cut back on bingo because St. John's in Seymour was complaining," tribal chairman Purcell Powless told the

Press-Gazette years later. "I told him to send a formal letter, but he never did."[8]

Congressman Cornell received a letter in the fall of 1977 from a constituent, Mrs. Joan Staley, who inquired whether federal law governed bingo games on Indian reservations and whether federal legislation might be created to subject Indian tribes to state laws. Congressman Cornell forwarded the inquiry in a November 30, 1977, letter to the Solicitor's Office for the Department of the Interior. Thomas Fredericks, associate solicitor, Division of Indian Affairs, responded on February 2, 1978, and told Cornell that there was no substantive federal criminal statute governing bingo games on Indian reservations, although gambling devices such as slot machines were illegal. Furthermore, Fredericks wrote, Wisconsin's Bingo Control Act could not be applied to the reservation based on the recent Supreme Court decision in *Bryan v. Itasca County.*[9]

That case originated after Minnesota's Itasca County had sent a $149.75 tax bill in 1972 to Russell Bryan, whose mobile home was on the Leech Lake Indian Reservation. He and his wife couldn't afford to pay the tax and asked tribal Legal Services for help. The Supreme Court reversed the lower courts' rulings and held that Public Law 280 did not cover taxation authority or matters of civil regulation on tribal property.

"Although it would be possible to enact federal legislation subjecting the Oneida tribe to state bingo laws, we do not recommend such an approach," Fredericks said in the letter to Cornell. "Similar problems to those described by Mrs. Staley exist in communities along Wisconsin's borders." Iowa and Minnesota charities near the Wisconsin border could not offer prizes as large as those as charities in Wisconsin. Wisconsin charities near the borders of Illinois and Michigan could not offer prizes as large as charities in those states, he wrote.

"Such disparities are an inevitable result of allowing each jurisdiction to make its own laws," Fredericks wrote. "We do not believe the inconvenience caused by such disparities justifies undermining self-government by imposing a federal solution."[10]

Nevertheless, Wisconsin officials began investigating the Oneida Bingo operation as a violation of state law. On July 25, 1979, Wisconsin Bingo Control Board inspector Ed Hughes investigated a bingo game at Oneida and later referred the matter to the Brown County district attorney for prosecution, according to a court affidavit.[11]

"There were a few times we thought the state might come in and shut us down," Sandy remembered. "A state inspector came in to look around and ask questions. We called him the Colonel because he looked like Colonel Sanders. He was heavy, round, and wore a fedora hat."

Native nations were beginning to find the sale of tobacco products a new area of tribal sovereignty to tap as well, and the sale of untaxed cigarettes caused additional conflict with state governments. The Florida Seminole tribe in 1977 began selling discount cigarettes from a drive-in booth along the busiest road through the reservation. Without the state's $2.10-per-carton tax, they were the cheapest cigarettes around.

The Oneida saw the potential in selling tax-free cigarettes to customers on their reservation. At a special Oneida Business Committee meeting November 29, 1978, the tribe enacted the Oneida Tobacco Ordinance regulating the sale of untaxed cigarettes on the reservation. The ordinance stated that all revenue derived from sales go to the Oneida tribe and be used exclusively for tribal public purposes. The tribe and the state Department of Revenue worked out a tax rule that allowed the sale of untaxed cigarettes to tribal members. An issue not settled was how many cigarettes were sold to non-Indians on the reservation. That issue was a point of contention with the state. The Business Committee also authorized the sale of cigarettes during bingo games at the gym. Mark Powless and Edwin King volunteered to staff a concession stand, according to meeting minutes.

"Ed King and my dad went to a [Great Lakes Intertribal Council] meeting in an old station wagon that had been donated to the tribe," said Purcell's daughter Bobbi Webster. "It was the first tribal chairman's car, a turquoise blue station wagon. I think it had bullet holes in the side. They bought cigarettes on that trip and came back and sold them."

The Oneida tribe began selling cigarettes in April 1979 from the Oscar Archiquette Building at Site I in Oneida. The price was $5.50 a carton, about $1 less than in stores. After just one month the operation posted $10,000 in gross sales, according to Ernest Stevens Sr., who at the time was manager of Oneida Tobacco Enterprises. "It's pretty lucrative. The idea has a lot of pizzazz to it," Ernest Sr. said in a June 9, 1979, *Green Bay Press-Gazette* story. "I'd put a Goodyear blimp over Green Bay and parachute out with a cigarette in my mouth if that's what it takes to sell them."

Ernest Jr. said he remembers seeing his dad coming out of Site I in a beat-up pickup truck going up the hill with a stack of cigarette cartons piled precariously high in the back. "It was nearly tipping over. He was just determined," Ernest Jr. told me. "My dad said sometimes it's just about getting people jobs. He always said as many jobs as we can create in this environment is just as important as the economic dollars that the business brings in."

The Oneida tribe opened a tobacco warehouse and retail outlet on November 10, 1979, on the tribe's industrial park land near West Mason Street and Lewellen Road with five employees. The senior Stevens told the *Kalihwisaks* that cigarette sales were being used for tribal operations and economic development. Proceeds were plowed back into inventory.

The legality of the tobacco sales continued to be questioned by the state, however. The *Press-Gazette* story on Oneida tobacco sales also noted that bingo was "another successful tribal business enterprise not subject to state law." New projects, conflicts, tension, profits: all were on the rise in Oneida.

Oneida's higher jackpots with bingo and sales of lower-priced cigarettes "were making for a sticky situation with the state," L. Gordon McLester III told me. "There was concern. Nobody really knew what they [the state] would do or could do." In addition to bingo and cigarettes, there was controversy over pull-tab instant lottery tickets, and the state raided Indian reservations that had gaming machines. Oneida did not have slot machines but was looking into casino games called Class III gaming. Class III games include slot machines, blackjack, craps, and roulette. There was some anxiety about whether bingo would be raided and individuals would be arrested. "Nobody had an answer," Gordon said.

Regardless of the legal trouble, the tribe was hard-pressed financially. Bingo was helping provide revenue.

The Bingo Committee, consisting of Sonny King, Alma Webster, Audrey Doxtator, Sandy Ninham, and Pat Misikin, had met on June 7, 1979, to discuss, among other things, what to do with the bingo money that was accumulating. In one move, the committee extended a ten-thousand-dollar loan at 12 percent interest to Oneida Tobacco Enterprises for another ninety days, Audrey's minutes said. The money would be used to buy more inventory.

Alma also suggested the Bingo Committee seriously think about paying off the mortgage on the tribal-owned Iroquois Farms at this time. "We will be able to save enough for a down payment on a new bingo building by the time we need it," Audrey's minutes said. Sandy seconded; all were in favor. The committee members agreed they would like to be there when the mortgage payoff took place, but no one wanted to buy land for a new building at this time. Pat Misikin said she'd check into possibilities as to how a new bingo building would fit into plans for tribal-owned sites at the airport and industrial park.

Three weeks later, at the June 28, 1979, meeting, the Bingo Committee members recommended loaning the tribe up to thirty-three thousand dollars to apply toward negotiations for buying land near the airport for a new building. The loan was interest free and repayable however and whenever the tribe decided, they said in the memo to the Business Committee. It was signed by Sandy Ninham, Pat Misikin, Alma Webster, and Audrey Doxtator. By late summer 1979, the bingo building fund had reached an amount sufficient to purchase a new site and provide an ample down payment on a new building.

At the Bingo Committee's August 15 meeting, the group discussed what to do with one hundred thirty thousand dollars that had been saved in bingo funds. Loretta Metoxen of the Business Committee also attended. The committee agreed to keep thirty thousand dollars for the building fund and allocate one hundred thousand dollars toward farmland acquisition and nursing home debt. Alma moved that 15 percent of all bingo proceeds be used in a special fund for land acquisition. This would not impact the present building fund, according to the minutes. All were in favor.

Unfortunately, a deep financial crisis confronted the tribe in late 1979. Some federal grant funding was ending and several tribal programs ran deficits. The bingo fund was exhausted that winter paying outstanding bills, according to an economic development plan written in October 1980 by senior tribal planner Carl Rasmussen and community planner Bruce Shaepe.

"I remember when we gave the tribe all the money we had saved—it was about a hundred and fifty thousand dollars," Sandy told me. "We said, 'You know what we just did? We paid the bills.' We realized we were covering the bills of the tribe."

The 1980 report also said the tribe's fiscal operations were overhauled in the wake of the financial crisis. A new IBM System 34 computer was installed in the accounting office to better track the financial status of programs. By the spring of 1980, the bingo building fund was growing once again, the report said.

Bingo and tobacco were providing a steady income source for the tribe. The 1980 economic report also cited recent gains in population and employment on the reservation, although bingo did not provide direct employment, since all workers were ostensibly volunteers. Nevertheless, tribal members living on or near the reservation rose from about 1,200 in 1960 to about 3,200 in 1980. In March 1978, Oneida unemployment was 21.7 percent. By 1980 the Oneida jobless rate had dropped to 17.7 percent, according to the BIA Labor Force Report, which was cited in the October 1980 economic development plan.

"Though the percentage is still far above the 6.1 percent rate for July 1980 in Brown County, it indicates that progress is being made. But the Oneida Nation has a long way to go to be comparable with the local economy of the surrounding area," the tribal economic report said.[12]

As building director, Sonny King gave monthly reports to the Business Committee about the civic center's activities and use. But Sonny was not directly involved in operating bingo games. The women were. Concerns over the bingo operation were directed toward the women managers.

At about this time, tribal chairman Purcell Powless began referring to the members of the Bingo Committee as the "bingo queens" when they appeared at tribal council meetings. Most people referred to bingo supervisors as "the bingo ladies." The term "lady" connotes a polite and proper woman, while "queen" refers to a woman monarch who rules in her own right, a female sovereign. The new nickname was a tongue-in-cheek acknowledgment of their growing power. It also underscored how bingo could become an economic development game-changer for the tribe.

"It was a turning point for the tribe. People saw the impact bingo had in helping programs and supplementing federal funding," Debbie

(Skenandore) Doxtator, who worked the kitchen during bingo and later was a grants writer for the tribe, told me. Once bingo began paying workers in the late 1970s, Debbie was able to buy her first car with her paycheck from working the kitchen at bingo.

There may have been an element of Indian sarcasm, however, in calling the bingo managers "queens," Chaz Wheelock told me. The nickname may have indicated that the women were acting like queens by assuming more authority than they were due. The Business Committee "wasn't always happy with us," Alma told me. But the Bingo Committee members no doubt felt they ought to have a say in the use of the money they had earned. Alma told me that women ran bingo "because it was women who played bingo." But plenty of men enjoyed playing bingo, too.

To some, the bingo managers were wielding power like the queen pieces on a chess board. In chess, the queen is the most powerful piece on the board. The king is the most important piece, however, as the game is over with checkmate—literally, "when the king is dead." But the queen can be the most domineering player because she can outmaneuver the other pieces. She can move any number of spaces, in any direction. The queen can move straight like a rook and diagonally like a bishop. She can do almost anything she wants except jump. Like an old man with a cane, the king can move only one space at a time. He will defend her at all costs. She's key to his survival. A queen sacrifice is a deliberate move in which the queen is forfeited for the benefit of the end game. But with his partner gone, the king might think, there is no love interest left in the game.

The game of chess developed and spread throughout medieval Europe much like bingo's precursor, the Italian lotto game. But Oneida was no medieval court populated with aristocracy. People in Oneida were concerned with simply surviving. Plenty of political maneuvering was going on in late 1979 as Oneida leaders surveyed the changing landscape in Wisconsin with regard to bingo, tobacco, and cultural survival.

Establishment of a tribal school was part of growing sovereignty efforts in Oneida. Late August 1979 saw the dedication of the new Oneida tribal school at Sacred Heart Center. The event held strong sentiment for many elders. The center, currently owned by the Green Bay Diocese and leased for use to the tribe, was on the site of the Oneida boarding school that educated Oneida children until its closing in 1919. The site, after sixty years, was once again a place for educating Oneida youths in Oneida ways. The Oneida tribal school opened on September 10 with Jerry M. Hill as its first principal. Hill was instrumental in developing the school's culturally based curriculum.

"We need to prepare our young people for the complexity of the world. We have lived 450 years of pretty unusual circumstances and we are still here," Hill told the crowd at the school's dedication.[13]

While bingo thrived in Oneida under the reign of female monarchs, more challenges were ahead. Conflict with state officials was on the rise, as was conflict inside the tribe. These battles usually came to a head in the tribal chairman's office in the old Chicago Corners building.

Purcell Powless had grown up in Oneida, served in the merchant marine in World War II, worked as an ironworker based in Chicago and Milwaukee, then moved back to Oneida to serve in tribal politics. Purcy, who was just over six feet tall, had been chairman twelve years by this time, since 1967. "He held the tribe together. He was polite, respectful, and friendly," recalled longtime Menominee leader and political activist Ada Deer. She remembered his modest office as a tiny room with one or two chairs and a school table for a desk. The furniture was likely government surplus or donated. He kept a dish of almonds or cashews on his desk, and an ashtray for his occasional cigar.

The tribe acquired the former two-room schoolhouse at Fish Creek Road and Outagamie County Road H after the Seymour School District closed the school. In 1975, the tribe remodeled the old Chicago Corners schoolhouse into offices for the tribal chairman, attorney, manager, and accountant. The Business Committee often held its meetings at Chicago Corners. While tribal actions were based on governing by consensus, meetings often became rancorous.

Some people in the community were said to foster a "crabs in the bucket" mentality. The phrase refers to crabs that could easily escape the confines of a bucket if they worked together and helped each other, but instead they pull each other back and no one gets out. The behavior typifies those who resent seeing anyone else succeed. "There were bitter tribal meetings," recalled attorney Jerry Hill. People would verbally attack each other. As chairman, however, Purcell Powless was able to keep the peace at these meetings. People often complained to him about others and would try to get him on their side. But Purcell stayed neutral until he heard from the other side.

Purcell often asked for a second opinion. "That would tick off the attorneys," said Rick Hill, son of Norbert Hill Sr. In 1976, Rick became the youngest person elected to the Business Committee. He was twenty-three.[14]

Others told me of at least one incident when a tribal member criticized the Business Committee's performance. Purcell turned it around and asked why that same critic had been seen drinking away his paycheck in taverns when he should have been supporting his children.

"Purcell was not formally educated, but he was very smart," Jerry Hill said. "He was practical and down to earth. He would ask questions but never really argue. He wanted to know why. Purcell always listened."

Purcell's daughter Bobbi Webster remembered her father's words to some of the tribal consultants and professionals. "'You've got the education, you figure it out. All the degrees in the world can't replace a doctorate from the school of hard knocks.' He'd say it to their faces," she recalled.

"He was a strong individual in the sense he took no guff from anybody," Sandy said. "If you got snippy, he'd be blunt with you. You couldn't pull the wool over his eyes." Sandy told me that Purcell once overheard her making a critical comment to someone about an old and slow janitor who worked at Chicago Corners. "He told me to be careful talking like that. He said that that janitor was so-and-so's father and was related to this person here and that person over there," Sandy said. "I was young. I was unaware of those extended families, extended kinships."

Rick Hill also recalled that Purcell often had to deal with a lot of bull. Purcell had little patience when cattle from the tribe's Iroquois Farms got loose and wandered onto roads. In April 1979, some cows escaped and a loose bull was shot. Purcy was outraged. "Well, they're Indian cows. They're going to get loose," Rick Hill recalled telling him.[15]

Purcell Powless was born December 25, 1925, to Mark and Margaret (Stevens) Powless in the homestead that had been allotted to his grandfather, John D. Powless. Purcell's father served as tribal chairman for a year in 1939. Purcell was one of nine children. Depression times forced his parents to send him to Pipestone Indian School in Minnesota and then to Flandreau Indian School in South Dakota, where he graduated. At age seventeen, in 1943, he joined the US Merchant Marine and traveled around the world, delivering lend-lease locomotives to Russia, food and clothing to England, and munitions to the Philippines.[16]

At one South Pacific port, he met some Maori tribesmen. "They looked like Indians. They thought I was one of them," Purcell said in a video interview. "What are you doing on a Yankee ship?" they asked him.[17]

After the war, he returned to Oneida and married Angeline Skenandore in 1946. Steady jobs were hard to find in this area. "Things were tough enough for white people, let alone Indians," Purcell told the *Press-Gazette* in 1984. He worked seasonal construction, picked peas, and unloaded pulp wood at the Green Bay docks. Then his brother John called to say there was construction work in Davenport, Iowa.

"My aunt gave me the money to get there," he said. Bethlehem Steel had brought in thirty to forty Mohawk from Montreal to erect high steel. Purcell was digging ditches when he was asked what he was doing on the ground. "You should be up there with them. Go down to the union hall and say you want to apprentice with the Mohawks," he was told.[18]

The Powless brothers rose from day laborers to skilled high-steel workers with the help of other Indians, particularly Mohawks, another tribe of the Iroquois League. "That's how we got into iron work," he said in the interview. With the help of the Mohawk crew, Purcell and John learned how to work on high-steel rivet gangs. Their brothers Eugene and Mark also apprenticed and later worked high steel. There was not much of that work around Green Bay, however. To get iron work, you had to belong to the union, so Purcell took his family with him as his jobs moved between Rock Island, Chicago, Milwaukee, and other locations around the Midwest. In 1955, he and brothers John and Mark worked on a crew building the Mackinac Bridge. A Mohawk rivet gang out of Detroit worked on one tower and the Oneida gang on the other, five hundred feet above the water through the windy Straits of Mackinac. The Mohawk men tried to get the Oneida gang to race them to see who was fastest. "We tried to keep pace with them, but not race," Purcell said in the video.

He and Angeline had five sons and three daughters: Richard, Greg, Ralph, Jamie, Joey, Kathy, Bobbi, and Monica. "We were born all over. I was born in Milwaukee," Bobbi said. "He took us as a family wherever he went."

Purcell was working in downtown Chicago when race riots in the early

1960s made things rough, so he moved his family back to Oneida. The family stayed put in Oneida and Purcell traveled. They moved into a home with no plumbing on unpaved Old Seymour Road. It had a woodstove and an outhouse.

Angeline was in charge of raising the family. "He'd come back from work filthy dirty. She'd hang the laundry on the line and in winter it would freeze. He'd take the train to Chicago from downtown Green Bay, where Titletown Brewing is now, or sometimes he'd drive. My mom didn't drive that often," Bobbi said.

At a picnic in Oneida in 1967, Norbert Hill Sr. urged him to run for Oneida tribal chair. He won. Serving with him were vice chairman Oscar Archiquette, treasurer Joy Ninham, and secretary Loretta Metoxen. The pay was five dollars per monthly meeting. The Oneida Nation had very little money at the time, before bingo. Unemployment was high on the reservation, and the tribe relied on federal funds and grants to provide services. People bought food on credit. They charged groceries at Schroeder's and Morgan's stores.

"He always said, 'I couldn't do this without my wife. We didn't have any latchkey children, thanks to Angie.' She raised us kids," said Bobbi Webster. "Mom instilled the values that we were responsible for our actions. Don't ever be vindictive. If someone does you wrong, show them the right way." Bobbi said her dad was at a corner tavern in Oneida one winter night when another man, who was intoxicated, became angry and upset with Purcell. Angie took Purcell home. Later that night, they saw the drunk man's car pass their house and slide off the road into a ditch. They waited and watched. No one got out.

"Let that sumbitch freeze," Bobbi said.

"No, you can't be that way," her mom told her. They helped him out of the car and made sure he got a ride home.

"After that he was always real nice to us," Bobbi said. "Treat people how you'd like to be treated. She tried to instill that in us kids."

In 1969, the elected body changed from a four-member to a nine-member council, and terms extended from one to three years. "There was still no money in it," Purcell told historian L. Gordon McLester III. Purcell continued to work on steel construction jobs to make ends meet and returned home for tribal meetings once a month. He worked on the Sears Tower in Chicago in 1970 with his brother Mark, and on Chicago's Ohio Street drawbridge.

"I think my mom was worried about him. But it never occurred to us kids he was in a dangerous job," said Bobbi. She recalled that her dad once fell on his back and was hospitalized in Chicago. "When my mom got that phone call, that was the worst thing. 'Don't take him,' I remember she said."

Purcell Powless said he learned from his union experience the importance of not burning any bridges with bosses. "You never want to eat crow. Sometimes you have to go back and work for them whether you like it or not. I learned that from the union," he said.[19]

Milton "Milt" Rosenberg, who was director of the Indian Law Center at the University of Wisconsin Law School at Madison, told me he first met Purcell at an intertribal meeting in 1977. In his job providing legal help to Wisconsin tribes, Milt also became acquainted with Oneida tribal attorneys Francis Skenandore and Jerry Hill starting about 1978.

"I had read a book called *Apologies to the Iroquois,* by Edmund Wilson," Milt told me. "Part of the book was devoted to a community of Mohawk on Staten Island who did much of the high-rise steel work," said Milt, whose family was from New York. "My father had told me of his awe at watching men standing on girders pitching red-hot rivets twenty stories up, and my respect only increased when I learned that those Mohawks in the book were probably the very men my father was talking about. Later I learned that Purcy had worked in high steel, and immediately the stereotype I had of such men went into effect."

Wilson's book includes a study of "The Mohawks in High Steel" by Joseph Mitchell, an article that had appeared in the *New Yorker* in 1949. Mitchell wrote that the high-steel Mohawk workers were from the Caughnawaga Reservation on the St. Lawrence River near Montreal, Quebec, and that colonies of Caughnawaga had spread to Brooklyn, Buffalo, and Detroit.

The Caughnawaga, known as the Christian Mohawks, originated in the late seventeenth century when French Jesuit missionaries persuaded dozens of Iroquois families in what is now New York State to settle a mission outpost in Quebec. The converts began arriving in 1668 and drew from all five nations of the Iroquois Confederacy at that time: the Mohawk, Oneida,

Onondaga, Cayuga, and Seneca. There also were a few Huron, Erie, and Ottawa who had been captured and adopted by the Haudenosaunee. The Mohawk predominated and so Mohawk customs and dialect became that of the whole group, Mitchell wrote. The Mohawk named their village *Ka-na-wa-ke*, which means "at the rapids." Caughnawaga is the latter-day spelling. The group retained much of the Haudenosaunee ways while adapting to new surroundings. Young men took jobs in the French fur trade handling freight canoes and later as proficient timber-raft runners over the rapids. In 1886, the Dominion Bridge Company (DBC) began building a cantilever railroad bridge across the St. Lawrence River near Caughnawaga. In obtaining rights to use reservation land for a bridge abutment, the bridge company promised that the Caughnawaga would be employed on the job wherever possible.[20]

The Indians, given jobs as day laborers unloading materials, were dissatisfied. Mitchell quoted from a letter written by a DBC official who said the Indians would climb up into the spans and walk around. They were inquisitive about the riveting and asked foremen if they could take a crack at it.

"This happens to be the most dangerous work in all construction, and the highest paid. Men who want to do it are rare and men who can do it are even rarer, and in good construction years there are sometimes not enough of them to go around," the bridge company official wrote. The company decided that training a group of them would be mutually advantageous. It is believed that the company initially trained twelve Mohawk ironworkers, enough to form three riveting gangs. After the DBC completed the railroad bridge, it began work on a bridge in Sault Ste. Marie, Michigan. Caughnawaga riveting gangs went along, taking apprentices with them. As soon as one apprentice was trained, the Mohawk workers would send back to the reservation for another one. Soon there'd be enough men for a new Indian gang, and a couple of the new ones would go into old gangs. By the early 1900s, Caughnawaga gangs were working on bridges and skyscrapers in New York and elsewhere across the country. They took up residences in the United States and returned to the reservation whenever they could for vacation or retirement.[21]

Milt told me he felt Purcell Powless had been forged of the same material as the Mohawk ironworkers he had read about. "I thought of Purcy as someone with great self-confidence and personal pride, who probably didn't need to be a blowhard to find personal satisfaction and a sense of achievement. That was the stereotyped impression I formed of Purcy thirty years back, and nothing I learned from personal dealings with him or the comments of my friends Francis and Jerry ever caused me to revise or change my estimation over the last thirty years," Milt said.[22]

Over the next few years, Purcell Powless and the three lawyers would find themselves facing shared conflicts that tested their resolve. Purcell, the toughened ironworker, never lagged in defending the women he called "our bingo queens."

Notes

1. Ada Deer, interview with the author, July 2011, Oneida, WI.
2. Eva Danforth served as Oneida tribal secretary from 1958 to 1963. Her son, James Danforth, served as the first chief of the Oneida Police Department from 1985 to 2003. Another son, Gerald Danforth, served as Oneida tribal chairman from 1999 to 2002 and again from 2005 to 2008.
3. Purcell Powless, Oneida Elder Interview with L. Gordon McLester III, Oneida Cultural Heritage Department, 2003.
4. "Oneida: A Nation Emerges," *Green Bay Press-Gazette*, December 9, 2001.
5. Oneida Business Committee meeting minutes of June 15, 1978, as reported in the July 7, 1978, issue of *Kalihwisaks*.
6. Mary Mullin, interview with the author, February 2010, Ashwaubenon, WI.
7. Father Robert J. Cornell, a Norbertine priest, represented northeastern Wisconsin's Eighth District in the US House of Representatives from 1975 to 1979. A Democrat from De Pere, he was only the second Catholic priest elected as a voting member of Congress. He taught at St. Norbert and Abbot Pennings high schools and St. Norbert College in De Pere. He also was known for promoting rock and country music shows in the 1960s and 1970s. He was defeated for re-election in 1978 by Republican Toby Roth. His plans to run again in 1980 ended when Pope John Paul II issued a ban on priests serving in elective office. The ban also ended the career of the other priest-congressman, Father Robert J. Drinan, a

Massachusetts Democrat who served five terms in Congress. Father Cornell died at St. Norbert Abbey in De Pere in 2009 at age eighty-nine.

8. "Oneida: A Nation Emerges," *Green Bay Press-Gazette*, December 10, 2001.

9. *Bryan v. Itasca*, 426 U.S. 373 (1976).

10. Thomas Fredericks, letter to US Rep. Robert J. Cornell, February 2, 1978, case file of *Oneida Tribe v. Brown County Sheriff Norb Froelich*, US District Court, Western District of Wisconsin, 81C54.

11. Peter Naze, affidavit, case file of *Oneida Tribe v. Brown County Sheriff Norb Froelich*.

12. "Overall Economic Development Plan Update, 1980–82," Oneida Tribe of Indians of Wisconsin, October 1980. The Indian population and employment statistics cited were released each March in the BIA Labor Force Report.

13. *Kalihwisaks*, August 31, 1979. The newspaper also reported the Oneida Hymn Singers opened the dedication. A prayer and welcoming session with a round dance followed. Chairman Purcell Powless also addressed the group. "We have to compete in two worlds and we want to give our children the best," Purcell said. Paul A. Skenandore added: "Your grandparents had to put up with many terrible things and the generations before them faced extreme odds for their existence. Now we can say the youth don't have it so bad."

14. Purcell Powless video tribute, Oneida Nation Museum, 2010.

15. Ibid.

16. "Purcell Powless: Oneida Leader Wants Only the Best for His Tribe," *Green Bay Press-Gazette*, August 2, 1984.

17. Purcell Powless, Oneida Elder Interview with L. Gordon McLester III, Oneida Cultural Heritage Department, 2003.

18. Ibid.

19. Ibid.

20. Joseph Mitchell, "The Mohawks in High Steel," in *Apologies to the Iroquois*, by Edmund Wilson (New York: Farrar, Straus & Giroux, 1959), pp. 3–36.

21. Ibid.

22. Milton Rosenberg, interview with the author, November 2010, Madison, WI.

CHAPTER 6

The Lawsuit and the Raid in Waiting

As SHE was setting up for a Sunday afternoon bingo game in November 1979, Sandra Ninham stepped outside the gym and glanced through the civic center lobby's glass doors to see if any police cars had pulled up at the reservation housing project.

Nothing. But plenty of bingo players were arriving on this fall day.

On most weekends a line of cars from Green Bay backed up on two-lane Highway 54 waiting to turn into the Site I housing project near Duck Creek. Kids' bikes and summer toys still dotted some front yards in the housing project in November, even though gray skies and bare trees meant winter wasn't far away. Men wearing heavy coats directed cars entering Site I to a parking lot that sloped from the back of the Oneida Nation Memorial Building down to tree-lined Duck Creek.

The dirt parking lot was graded that spring to fit the growing number of bingo players. Parking attendants packed the one-hundred-parking-space lot tightly with Chevy trucks, AMC Pacers, Dodge Aspens, Datsun pickups, and Ford vans. But even with the expanded parking, many cars still had to be parked along the streets in front of the HUD-built duplexes. Later that winter, bingo managers would ask parking attendants not to let players park in front of the housing units for the elderly in Site I because the Oneida Hymn Singers met at Melinda Doxtator's apartment on Sunday afternoons and some elders had a hard time walking very far.[1]

Inside the gray concrete civic center, cash would be flying as furiously as the dry leaves blowing outside in the November wind. By the end of the night, the floor was strewn with discarded bingo papers and pull-tab raffle tickets.

Regular players like Shirley Czech knew to come early or risk being turned away when the hall filled up. Lately, charter buses had been showing up, carrying gamblers from Manitowoc and Milwaukee.

Alma Webster often sat at a table collecting entry fees in a wooden box. Her teenage son, Don, and daughters Melissa and Susan usually worked the floor. Other young people took turns acting as caller. Sandra Ninham was usually at the microphone, supervising giveaways and door prizes and keeping an eye on her five kids, who ranged in age from four to seventeen. Sandy's daughter Pamela, then fourteen, remembers she regularly brought her youngest brother, Matthew, to bingo for an hour or so. He'd wear his favorite outfit of cowboy boots and a blue vest, Pamela recalled.

Audrey Doxtator and Lillian King were the other bingo supervisors who oversaw about thirty-five Oneida workers, some of them their own children or kids who lived in Site I. If a raid happened, the young workers knew they wouldn't be the ones arrested, but they'd be out of a job.

Sandy arrived early at the gym on Sunday mornings, about 8 a.m. In between sessions, she'd do her family's wash in the center's laundry machines. She had a washer and dryer at home but was rarely there to use them. The civic center was becoming like a second home, a place to play, work, and socialize.

"Grandpa Don and Bob and Millie Schultz from Manitowoc liked to come early to help set up tables and sell packets of cards," Sandy recalled.

At first, the Boys' Club, under the supervision of Rick Hill, ran the kitchen, serving sandwiches and coffee. Later, Brenda and Debbie Skenandore took their place.

By 1979, Oneida Bingo had replaced the old hand-cranked cage filled with bingo balls with an air-blow machine. The new machine was set on a raised platform and whirled seventy-five numbered balls marked from B-1 to O-75. The caller picked out each ball funneled into a chute, held it up, and called the number through a microphone.

"Bee-ah nine-ah," the caller said, exaggerating the pronunciation for better audio effect. The ball also was posted on a flashboard behind the caller. Each session of Oneida Bingo, typically lasting about four hours, consisted of thirty-four games. Winners of most games got $20 apiece. Then the jackpot began to rise, with between $20 and $40 for the fifth game, $100 awarded for the tenth game, $125 for the twentieth game, and $150 for the thirtieth. Games in between paid $20. The thirty-fourth and final game of the session was a progressive blackout, which paid $500 or more if it was claimed by the fifty-third ball being called.

Cash wasn't the only prize. One November afternoon, bingo organizers arranged for twenty-five frozen turkeys to be given away as prizes. For the lucky winners, this Thanksgiving was on the Indians.

The supervisors who served on the Bingo Committee back then—Sandy, Alma, Audrey, and Lillian—were aware that if police raided the tribal operation, they likely would be the ones arrested. What they weren't aware of until years later was that a group of broad-shouldered Oneida men, the so-called red-bandanna boys, were prepared to block the doorways if police tried to shut down the bingo operation.

A confrontation appeared likely, tribal lawyer Francis Skenandore recalled. The red-bandanna boys told Skenandore that they could be there outside the gym if given fifteen minutes' notice that a raid was imminent. If a raid occurred it was possible someone could get hurt. Francis gave me the names of two of the red-bandanna boys, twin brothers David and Dennis Danforth.

I got in touch with Dennis, who's been working in construction since about 1980. He and David have been active in Oneida language programs and in Buffalo Creek Singers at powwows, socials, and ceremonies. Dennis and David credited their schooling at Flandreau Indian School in Flandreau, South Dakota, as a turning point in their lives. At Flandreau, they learned to focus on traditional Indian ways and put aside mainstream vices. Their growing cultural awareness was a source of self-esteem and self-confidence. Indian boarding schools, which had been designed originally to assimilate Indians, had evolved over time into centers for instilling Indianness.

Dennis graduated from high school in 1976 and was an accomplished amateur boxer. "At that time, people were beginning to understand we had culture. We were bringing our culture back to the community," Dennis told me.

I asked him about the red bandannas for which his group was named. "That's what we wore. It was normal for us. Like a hat," he said. Wearing the bandanna got him into at least one fight, with a man who told him, "You think you're tough," and tried to take a swing at him.

Dennis recalled there was talk of a possible raid on the bingo hall and a warning to be ready.

"We were active in those types of things, standing up for our rights," said Dennis. "It was an issue of sovereignty." He said their action was intended to be a peaceful protest, not violent. "We were not sure what to expect, so we had to be prepared for the worst-case scenario," he said.

No raid had happened yet. But by the end of 1979 tension was growing between tribal leaders and state agencies about whether an Indian bingo hall would have to comply with Wisconsin's bingo control law. A state bingo inspector came around Oneida Bingo in July of 1979 to gather evidence. On October 18 of that year, Brown County district attorney Peter Naze wrote to Wisconsin attorney general Bronson La Follette asking for an opinion as to whether the DA's office had the power to enforce the state's bingo control law on an Indian reservation.[2]

A Brown County assistant district attorney, Royce Finne, met with tribal leaders in Oneida that same month and warned them that bingo managers could face prosecution if they didn't comply with state law. The tribal leaders were told they could face up to nine months in jail or a $10,000 fine if convicted of the misdemeanor crime.[3]

Similar conflicts were developing on Indian reservations elsewhere at about the same time. In December 1979, the Seminole Tribe of Florida was making headlines over its plans to open a high-stakes bingo parlor along a highway in the Everglades near Hollywood, Florida. James Billie, who became the Seminole tribal chairman in June 1979, was handed a developer's proposal estimating that bingo could raise $3 million a year. He went forward with plans even though the tribe's attorney doubted it was legal under Florida law.

The Florida tribe was ready to launch its 1,200-seat high-stakes bingo hall, open daily with a jackpot of two thousand dollars. Broward County sheriff Robert Butterworth threatened to shut it down before the December 1979 opening because it would violate Florida's limit of twice-a-week sessions with the top prize capped at a hundred dollars. In Fort Lauderdale US District Judge Norman Roettger ruled in favor of the tribe and issued an injunction barring Sheriff Butterworth from interfering. Judge Roettger cited a Washington State case in which tribal members were convicted of selling fireworks on Indian land in violation of state law. Federal courts determined that the Washington violation was a criminal prohibition, not civil regulation. Since Florida permits some groups to hold bingo, the state had chosen to regulate, not prohibit, the activity, Roettger said in his ruling.[4] The Seminole bingo hall opened on December 14, 1979, and Butterworth appealed to the Fifth Circuit Court of Appeals.

The bingo managers in Oneida were concerned that if a raid shut down Oneida Bingo, several dozen young people would be out of part-time jobs and the tribe would be denied a source of revenue that financed needed social service programs.

With the new year of 1980, the tribe's Bingo Committee prepared to make its first semiannual financial report to the General Tribal Council, which is made up of all tribal members. The report showed that bingo raised more than a half million dollars for the tribe.

The report included a breakdown of money generated since bingo's start in 1976:

October–December 1976 . . . .$2,165.99

January–December 1977 . . . . . .$46,421.81

January–December 1978 . . . . .$151,841.11

January–December 1979 . . . . .$382,114.28

TOTAL $582,543.19

Expenditures for supplies $50,348.36

Net proceeds $532,194.83

"We employ between 30 and 40 people to work the games and help with cleanup. Most of these are the children of our community who have no other way of earning some extra spending money for their own small necessities," the report said. "People come from all over the state and tell us how good our game is and how good the workers are on the floor. We have the support of our regular customers when the state and various other organizations attempt to interfere with our game." The report was signed,

"Your Bingo Committee," with signatures by members Sandra Ninham, Alma Webster, Audrey Doxtator, and Lillian King. The fifth Bingo Committee member, Sonny King, had resigned in December 1979 and was replaced in February 1980 by Kathy Hughes.

The mention of groups attempting to "interfere with our game" was an understatement. On January 29, 1980, Wisconsin attorney general Bronson La Follette issued a formal opinion to District Attorney Naze saying that the Oneida tribe must comply with state regulation or face enforcement steps. "In the situation you have described, the Oneida Tribe has been conducting bingo games but has not applied for a bingo license under Chapter 163. Furthermore, the procedures used in awarding prizes appear to be in violation of Chapter 163. The issue is whether the state has jurisdiction over the bingo activities conducted by the Oneida Tribe," La Follette wrote.

Until 1973, bingo was considered a lottery prohibited by the state. Chapter 163 was enacted to implement the constitutional amendment permitting bingo games by certain groups licensed by the state for charitable purposes. It was La Follette's opinion that Congress, with passage of Public Law 280, authorized the state of Wisconsin to enforce its criminal laws in Indian country. "It is my opinion that unless the bingo operations on the Oneida Reservation can be brought into compliance with Chapter 163, the persons engaged in their conduct are subject to appropriate legal action by your office," La Follette wrote to Naze.

On February 1, 1980, Assistant District Attorney Finne wrote to Francis Skenandore about the opinion: "As you may recall from our earlier discussions, it is the opinion of this office" that the tribe must be brought into compliance on the bingo issue.

The news quickly made headlines. "Bingo on Indian Land May Become Legal Fight," the *Green Bay Press-Gazette* reported February 3, 1980. The story said La Follette had advised the county that individual Oneida could be prosecuted for conducting bingo without a license. It went on to say Oneida bingo games were questioned by charitable groups in the Green Bay area because the Oneida reportedly were drawing larger crowds by offering larger prizes than permitted by state law.

Robert Hoskins of Madison, a former state bingo commissioner acting as a spokesman for the local groups, was quoted in the February 3 *Press-Gazette* story as saying that the Oneida were awarding total prizes of two thousand dollars a session, exceeding the legal limit of one thousand dollars a session imposed on other groups. The Oneida also paid their workers, ran progressive jackpot games with accumulating proceeds, and sold pull-tab lottery-type tickets, all in violation of state law, Hoskins said in the interview.

The Oneida declined to comment on the issue in the press. But the story noted that Oneida tribal attorney Francis Skenandore told Finne in October the tribe maintained it had sovereignty over its activity on tribal land. The story said there was precedent for the Indian position in federal Department of the Interior opinions as recently as February 1978 and in previous La Follette opinions, including one in November 1976.

Finne was quoted as saying he was surprised by La Follette's latest finding, even though he could understand why other groups sponsoring bingo might have thought the situation unfair. Finne said he wrote Skenandore requesting that the operation be brought into compliance with state law.

"I assume he will respond. Everybody just wants them to comply. If they do, it's no problem. If not, it is a problem," Finne told the *Press-Gazette*.

Tribal lawyers Francis Skenandore and Jerry Hill and other tribal leaders on the Business Committee knew it would be a problem. They were intent on not backing down. Led by chairman Purcell Powless, they planned to stand up to the state and assert tribal rights.

The day after the newspaper story broke, the Business Committee held its regular monthly meeting. Francis Skenandore recommended that a memo be sent to all tribal employees telling them not to talk to the media concerning bingo operations or face termination. Vice chairman Norbert Hill made the motion and treasurer Wendell McLester seconded. The motion passed, according to meeting minutes. On February 5, Francis wrote a memo to the Business Committee calling La Follette's opinion a direct attack on the tribe's sovereignty, the right of the tribe to make its own laws and be governed by them.

"If this attack on tribal sovereignty is not taken seriously the tribe will be seriously weakened in any future power it may assert," Skenandore wrote. "Equally important is tribal support of the Oneida tribal members operating bingo for the tribe. They must be assured that what they are doing is done with the full support of the Oneida tribe for a tribal purpose."

I interviewed Francis later about that period.

"I give credit to the people who were willing to step forward and put themselves on the line," he told me. Was a raid coming? I asked.

"I can't say where the tip came from, but we got a warning that the sheriff was going to pull a raid," Francis said. "I advised the Business Committee what might happen. Our advice was not to shut down bingo. If those women were willing to put themselves at risk of arrest, we would defend them. Purcell said don't back down. He was a good person for the time."

Sandy Ninham's son Tim, a sixteen-year-old bingo worker at the time, recalled that Purcell told his mom not to worry about a police raid. "You handle the games. Let us worry about the state," Purcell told the bingo managers, according to Tim Ninham.

Francis said he called a county official to warn that if a raid happened there could be injuries. A number of Oneida men said they were prepared to block the doorway if deputies arrived. Two years earlier, some of the same young men and boys were upset that bingo was taking over the gym. Now they were among those willing to defend it.

"They were protective of us," Sandy said. "When the state threatened to raid the gym, they were there in the hallway. Those guys knew we were the source of the income that paid for baseballs, bats, and kids' uniforms."

Sandy told me the bingo managers were too busy running the games to worry about being arrested. Their biggest concern was drawing so many people that they had to turn them away.

The Bingo Committee, meanwhile, also held its meeting February 4. There was no mention in the minutes of the threat of a state raid. The committee decided it could use about four more tables and thirty-two more chairs for bingo. Sonny King said he'd look into getting them. Something also needed to be done about the smoke in the gym during bingo. The fan pulled out warm air in the winter and cool air in the summer, and it was thought a smoke filtration system would save on heating and cooling costs, according to minutes.

Three weeks later, at the Bingo Committee's February 28 meeting, the group approved paying floorworkers fifteen dollars if they worked early and late sessions. Sandy Ninham was elected Bingo Committee chair and Lillian King secretary.

"I remember when the state was after us and wanted to shut us down and arrest us," Sandy told me. "At a BC [Business Committee] meeting they asked us if we were willing to be arrested. It would go on our record and might affect our credit rating. They'd joke that if it took the rest of their lives and all the money in the tribe, they'd get us out of jail. They told us that all the time," Sandy said.

"That's how they dealt with it, by joking," Sandy's husband at the time, Lee Ninham, told me years later. Sandy said she wasn't worried about it, but Lee said he was. "I remember we talked about it. They couldn't touch the kids because they were minors. She knew the tribe's law office would have their backs."

For the Ninhams, the loss of Sandy's job wasn't a concern; Lee had a steady paper mill job in Green Bay. "It would have been a loss for the tribe if they shut it down," Lee said.

Bingo managers were concerned about the state confiscating supplies or equipment in a raid, so they moved items out of the civic center. They also didn't want customers punished, so they burned records containing names of winners.

"Pat Misikin, Alma, and I each took a box of papers. It took Lee three days to burn it in the backyard," Sandy said.

The prospect of bingo moms being led away in handcuffs while their children watched seemed a very real possibility. Yet neither side wanted to see an enforcement action that could blow up into a political conflict, former tribal attorney Jerry Hill told me in an interview.

"In his letter, Finne is saying what he has to say. I think they didn't want to do it because raids are very . . . cumbersome. You know, nobody looks good. It would be mainly white people they would be pushing around. If they were pushing around Indians that would be different or if it were an academic argument in which there was no excitement, that would be different. But when you get police out there and you start pushing them around and interfering with the games, that's very bad. That's bad PR. So we had to stand up to them. Naze understood that what we were setting up was a court battle instead of a confrontation," Jerry said.

"I think Naze really wanted it resolved. I don't think he really cared that we were having bingo. He just didn't want to be put in a position to enforce something that could erupt into a political conflict in which nobody looks good. They would look like a bunch of racists and we look like a bunch of obstructionists or law breakers. In the paper, it looked like we were anticipating a fight. But we decided a fight wouldn't get us what we wanted. What we wanted was to run bingo. We felt like if we could get it in court that we could win. That's what we intended. That was the strategy."

The 1970s had seen several cases of landmark occupations by Indian activists, most notably by the alliance called Indians of All Tribes, which occupied Alcatraz Island for nineteen months between 1969 and 1971. Hill had been a part of the Alcatraz occupation.

Born Gerald L. Hill in Oneida in 1936, Jerry grew up in Detroit where his father, Albert, a brother of Norbert Hill Sr., worked during the war. Jerry returned to Oneida in summers and stayed with his grandmother. At age seventeen, he joined the air force and was stationed at bases around the country, finally as a hydraulic aircraft mechanic in Riverside, California. He left the service after six years, married, and worked in aircraft factories and missile silos and tested rocket engines.

"For age twenty-four or twenty-five, it was kind of exciting," he said in a video interview with historian L. Gordon McLester III. He later went to beauty school and owned two salons in California. Then he quit that work, put his car in storage, and moved to Alcatraz, where he says he "got into the Indian business." By early 1970, the occupation began to fall into disarray. He soon found the occupation to be disorganized at best. "There seemed to be no one in charge. I tried to help out at the school. I babysat kids and read books with them. I stayed four months and finally snapped. Too much drinking, violence. It seemed there was no organization." Activists later said the occupation served its purpose by drawing attention to Indian problems and creating a movement.

Back in Los Angeles, Jerry was recruited to go to law school at the University of California–Davis. He spent two summers interning with the tribal government in Oneida in 1975–1976 and worked at the tribal building at Chicago Corners. There he found a table stacked with correspondence. It was mostly people fighting over land assignments. His uncle, Norbert Hill Sr., helped get him hired after graduation as a tribal attorney.[5]

Now nearly four years later, Jerry Hill and Francis Skenandore were facing a legal battle over tribal bingo. It appeared lawyers on both sides wanted it settled in court with no outside incidents.

Francis, meanwhile, was meeting regularly in Madison with Milt Rosenberg, the director of the Indian Law Center at the University of Wisconsin Law School. Francis and Milt would continue to talk legal strategy over lunches at the Copper Top and Hacienda restaurants in Madison through the 1980s and 1990s.

The fact that women already had a bingo hall in existence gave the Oneida's case greater weight than if they were trying to get one started, Milt told me in an interview.

"We felt this was a revenue stream worth defending," he said.

Milt, whose family came from New York, had taught philosophy at UW–Madison. He told me he became disillusioned with teaching and yearned for something more. He entered UW Law School and recalled he was studying landlord-tenant disputes when a lease problem in a Menominee Indian case captured his attention. He earned his law degree from UW in 1976 and started reading about Indian law cases at night. The UW Law School wanted to start an Indian Law Center and picked Milt to head it. The idea was to use Indian law students to do research, he said. Milt obtained a small grant to do summer outreach. He wrote legal briefs for tribal governments at no charge to them. "It was part of my duties," he said.

Milt saw that bingo could have a significant impact for Wisconsin tribes. If the Oneida won their case, the door would open for other tribes to start their own bingo operations, he said.

In September 1980, the state attorney general asked the tribe for an outline of the Oneida bingo ordinance to ascertain how the tribe was regulating the program. Oneida tribal officials wanted to make their case as sound as they could. They needed to prove in court that it was a tribe-run enterprise operated for the benefit of tribal members. The attorneys pushed for amending the Oneida bingo ordinance in October 1980, requiring that all workers be Indians enrolled in a tribe, and all bingo supervisors be enrolled Oneida members. That meant all non-Indian workers would be fired. Alma Webster later reported to the Business Committee that three paid workers who were non-Indians were terminated because of the new policy. It also meant non-Indian volunteers like Sandy's grandfather Don Barrett were no longer allowed to help. Don, her grandmother Celinda's second husband, was of Belgian heritage.

"When the ordinance was done, my Grandpa Don was told he couldn't help set up tables or sell packets anymore," Sandy said. "He was heartbroken. He felt really bad he couldn't help. I remember he went down the road crying. He was just a little man, but he loved doing it."

Attorney Jerry Hill said the reasoning behind only tribal members being allowed to work at bingo was that it was a tribal enterprise. "It benefits tribal members by providing work. We didn't want to mess up that argument," Jerry said.

The ban on volunteer labor also stemmed from liability insurance in which volunteers wouldn't be covered if they were injured. When hiring boomed in the late 1980s, the Indian-only requirement was dropped for many entry-level jobs. Top tribal management positions remain listed for enrolled Oneida only.

The Oneida weren't the only ones creating new revenue streams in 1980. The Cabazon Band of Mission Indians outside Indio, California, tried to raise revenue several ways that year. Its attempts at mail-order cigarettes and tax-free liquor sales were shut down due to federal regulations. That October the Cabazon opened a bingo and poker club. Days later police from the city of Indio raided the hall and arrested 102 employees and customers. A court backed the Cabazon in a narrow ruling that affected only the city. After the Cabazon reopened the club, Riverside County sheriff's deputies followed suit with another raid. They issued citations and impounded records and cash. Cabazon tribal officer Brenda James Soulliere, who was working the cashier's cage, recalled the second raid in Ambrose Lane's *Return of the Buffalo*.

"I was in the cage. I was just getting ready to leave and the other girl was coming on. All of a sudden, somebody shouted, and all of these green jackets came in, and I started to walk out. She started freaking out, 'What's going on? Don't leave!' . . . So I stayed there and then they were banging on the door to open the cage. . . . Finally, I opened the door. They came in and . . . òh, they went through my purse. I didn't like that idea. They confiscated the money and the chips and, I believe, I had to sign something of what they were taking. . . . They took our picture. We didn't really know what was going on. It's just that there were sheriffs everywhere taking all of our things. . . . We had to get an injunction to open back up," she said.[6]

Two months later, the Morongo tribe in Riverside County prepared to open its own bingo hall. Anticipating a raid, the Morongo filed a lawsuit. A federal judge consolidated the Cabazon and Morongo cases and the issue worked its way up the court system over the next six years.

The Seminole case, meanwhile, was being litigated in federal court in Florida when the Oneida decided they were willing to go to court over bingo. A similar principle was involved in the Seminole case.

On October 7, 1980, the Wisconsin attorney general's office wrote Brown County district attorney Naze with news of a ruling in the federal case of *Seminole Tribe of Florida v. Butterworth*. The court concluded Florida's statutes were primarily regulatory in nature—not prohibitory—and that Florida did not have authority to enforce regulatory laws against Indians on Indian land under Public Law 280.

"Please understand that I do not mean to suggest that the Attorney General is considering any changes [in his prior opinion]," assistant attorney general John Niemisto wrote to Naze. "I have brought the Florida case to your attention, however, because it is now on appeal and if the Court of Appeals affirms the lower court's decision, that could have some impact on how the courts would view the Wisconsin Bingo Control Act and its application to Indian bingo operations in Wisconsin."

Milt Rosenberg said that letter amounted to a warning that the state's position could fail. Each side, however, continued on its course, with the Oneida attorneys pressing ahead with a civil lawsuit aimed at preventing a raid and the state maintaining that federal law gave Wisconsin authority over Indian land.

"To start a suit we needed a cause of controversy," Francis Skenandore told me.

The tribe needed to show that the state intended to prosecute, Jerry Hill said. "We needed to show that it wasn't just our feeling that they were going to do something. It was an actual formal letter of what they were going to do. So I called [district attorney Peter Naze] and said we need a letter from you saying that you are going to follow the law." Naze worked with Brown County Sheriff Norbert Froelich on writing the letter so that it reflected the county's legal stance and came from the sheriff, the county's law enforcer. "So that was part of what we needed to file that lawsuit," Jerry said.[7]

On December 15, 1980, Sheriff Froelich's letter to tribal chairman Purcell Powless said he had received complaints of bingo on Oneida tribal grounds in violation of Wisconsin's bingo control law, Chapter 163, Wisconsin Statutes. Chapter 163 provides criminal penalties, a civil forfeiture, or imposition of a restraining order.

"Please be advised that unless the Oneida Tribe immediately ceases and desists from conducting bingo games, this department will enforce the law and seek one or more of the aforementioned remedies," Froelich's letter said.

The letter provided the cause of controversy the Oneida had been waiting for, and on January 20, 1981, the tribe filed a civil suit in US District
Court for the western district of Wisconsin in Madison. (The suit was filed
in the western district court because that was the location of the attorney
general, the main defendant.) In the suit the Oneida sought a preliminary
injunction against the defendants from interfering with or harassing bingo
operations. It was signed by Francis Skenandore, Gerald L. Hill, and Milton
Rosenberg. Defendants were the state of Wisconsin, attorney general Bronson La Follette, and the Wisconsin Bingo Control Board.

The suit contained four affidavits, or sworn statements, from Oneida officials in support of an injunction. Tribal chairman Purcell Powless stated
that the reservation suffered from unemployment two to three times that
of the surrounding community. Given the tribe's lack of a tax base, Oneida
Bingo made a major contribution toward providing services to tribal members. Suspending bingo would seriously harm the tribe, he said.

Sandra Ninham, chair of the Oneida Bingo Committee, said in her affidavit that all bingo proceeds were subject to appropriation solely by the
Oneida Business Committee for tribal purposes, and that no non-Indians
conducted, worked, or assisted in the bingo games. (That applied to her
own non-Indian friends and relative.)

Kathy Hughes, assistant controller for the tribe, said in her affidavit that
bingo revenues had been disbursed to the Oneida nursing home, tribal
school, Head Start, Agency on Aging, and youth programs.

The affidavit from Audrey Doxtator, director of the Oneida Community
Health Center, stated that bingo funds had made a vital contribution to
the construction of buildings and for providing comprehensive health care
services.

News of the suit was reported in the *Kalihwisaks* on January 30 under the
headline "Bingo Goes to Court." In his news column, Chairman's Corner,
Purcell Powless wrote that "the bingo game proceeds have helped to fund
elderly programs and social and civic activities. It is the only source of income that the tribe can count on to fund these programs."

The case was assigned to US District Judge Barbara Crabb. Judge Crabb
granted an expedited hearing on January 29, 1981, to hear arguments on the
Oneida tribe's motion for preliminary injunction. Appearing for the tribe at
the one-hour hearing were Jerry Hill, Francis Skenandore, Milt Rosenberg,

and Milt's assistant Fran Wells. Appearing for the state were Donald Johns and John Niemisto, according to court records.

Francis Skenandore knew the burden was on the tribe to show that the case would likely succeed on merits, that the tribe had no other remedy and would be irreparably harmed if the injunction were not issued. Furthermore, the tribe had to show that closing bingo would harm the tribe more than leaving it open would harm the state, and the granting of an injunction must not be a disservice to the public interest. Francis explained these details to the Business Committee the following week.

After listening to arguments from the tribe and the state, Judge Crabb took the matter under advisement, with a decision to be issued later. She did not set a time limit. The next week, on February 5, the judge wrote to the parties saying she had discovered one potential issue not addressed at the hearing. It appeared that threat of enforcement of bingo laws was coming from the sheriff and district attorney of Brown County. Yet no one from those offices was named in the lawsuit.

Milt Rosenberg replied on February 12 that the state specifically threatened to enforce its laws against Oneida bingo operations. Brown County was acting as an agent of the state under its advice. He said the tribe had omitted the county not to create problems but to address the controversy in the most direct fashion. "Litigation is better served by dealing with the governmental bodies who are the true parties to the controversy, especially in Indian cases, where the scope of Indian rights and immunities ought to be a matter of state rather than local policy," Milt wrote. Assistant attorney general John Niemisto told the court that the county district attorney had primary responsibility for enforcement of Wisconsin law and that the state had no objection to adding the county as defendant. The tribe followed the judge's suggestion and amended the suit in March to name Brown County sheriff Norbert Froelich as defendant, as well as district attorney Peter Naze. On February 18, the state filed a motion to dismiss the suit.

Nine days later, on February 27, Judge Crabb entered an order denying the tribe's motion for a preliminary injunction on the ground the tribe had failed to show that it would suffer irreparable harm from the defendants if the injunction were not granted.

The ruling appeared to be a setback for the tribe, but the case was not lost. In fact, the suit had accomplished what the tribe wanted. It stopped—for now—any enforcement action from occurring. The bingo hall remained open while the issue was being litigated. There would be no raid until the judge ruled.

The bingo queens could breathe easier. There would be no arrests for the moment.

In light of the pending court case, the *Green Bay Press-Gazette* ran a story May 17 on the big business of bingo in Brown County. The story said county residents spent more than five hundred thousand dollars on bingo cards in the preceding year and that Wisconsin residents spent $18 million statewide in the same period. Catholic church bingo games accounted for 32 percent of net profits in the county. Veterans groups, civic groups, and fraternal orders accounted for the rest. As a sovereign nation, the Oneida tribe did not report its take to the state. A *Press-Gazette* reporter, Keith Goldschmidt, attended one of the Oneida games. Goldschmidt wrote that at Oneida Bingo, the stakes were higher and the prizes bigger, and raffle tickets were sold by the handful to eager customers.

"It's a far cry from the somewhat tame games played at churches. It's a quicker, more electric game. It draws bigger crowds. It is played more often. And it pays in cash on the spot," Goldschmidt wrote. He estimated the Oneida paid out $2,600 to winners the night he attended and took in receipts of about $6,000. His estimate was based on a crowd of four hundred with the average person buying six regular cards, four special cards, and six raffle tickets. Most players appeared to buy more than that, he said.

Although good times prevailed inside the bingo palace, the heat was turning up elsewhere in the Oneida community. In early 1981 tribal chairman Purcell Powless, who had worked to defend the bingo queens, found himself under fire.

Some tribal members questioned the direction of the tribe after the 1979 financial crisis left some tribal programs with deficits. The $150,000 bingo building fund was exhausted on outstanding bills. The tribe wasn't alone in a crisis. The United States was experiencing higher unemployment and a lower gross domestic product between 1980 and 1982. The Federal Reserve tried to tighten the money supply to stem inflation, which jumped from 11.3

percent in 1979 to 13.5 percent in 1980. The federal funds rate, the interest rate at which depositories trade balances held at the Federal Reserve, rose from 11 percent in 1979 to 20 percent in June 1981. In April 1981, President Ronald Reagan announced cuts in federal programs, including some funding to Indian tribes. Federal planning grants had helped provide salaries to some Oneida tribal managers. The Oneida tribal chairman had been a full-time position since 1973, thanks in part to federal grants.

In the May 22, 1981, edition of *Kalihwisaks*, Purcell Powless wrote in his chairman's column that he was reducing his salary to half time because of the financial problems the tribe was having.

The chairman's salary was $22,500, the *Kalihwisaks* reported July 17, 1981. The vice chairman earned $18,000, treasurer $18,750, secretary $16,250, and five at-large council members $13,750 each.

Nineteen eighty-one was an election year for three-year terms on the Oneida Business Committee. Some people felt it was time for a change in leadership. Among those challenging Purcell for chairman were Gary Metoxen, a career navy veteran, Business Committee member Loretta Metoxen, and former *Kalihwisaks* editor Paul Skenandore.

In the tribal election on Saturday, July 25, Purcell Powless lost his chairman's position by just three votes. Gary Metoxen received 349 while Purcell received 346 votes, Loretta Metoxen 107, and Paul Skenandore 22.

Purcell requested a recount.

On July 27, 1981, the Monday after the election, Judge Crabb issued her opinion and order on the state's motion to dismiss the bingo lawsuit. At issue was Public Law 280, which granted limited civil and general criminal jurisdiction to the state over Indian country within Wisconsin.[8] The state argued that because the state's bingo laws provide a criminal penalty for bingo operators who do not comply with the law, the laws were "criminal" for purposes of jurisdiction under Public Law 280. But the judge concluded that the state bingo law was "civil regulatory" in nature and did not fall within the act's grant. Judge Crabb cited the Marshall-era Supreme Court decision of *Worcester v. Georgia*, which held that the state of Georgia could not enforce its laws on the Cherokee Reservation. Indian nations are dealt with exclusively by the federal government. Under this view, Indian tribes retained internal sovereignty unless overridden by Congress. Judge Crabb denied the state's motion to dismiss. Her ruling noted that once the state legalized bingo, it lost its regulatory jurisdiction under P.L. 280 on the Oneida reservation. She observed that "the Wisconsin legislature and the general populace, as evidenced by the constitutional amendment of 1973, have determined that bingo playing is generally beneficial and have chosen to regulate rather than prohibit."

Judge Crabb also noted that her interpretation of P.L. 280 appeared to be in keeping with present federal policy encouraging tribal self-government.

This was not her summary judgment, or final ruling, but it was a good indication of how she would rule. The tribe would win. "The judge's action seems to strongly suggest that she will rule in favor of the tribe," assistant attorney general John Niemisto told the *Press-Gazette* in a phone interview later that week.

News of the court's action did not prompt any celebration in the Oneida community, however. In fact, it went largely unnoticed. More people were concerned with that weekend's close tribal election result and what it would mean for the tribe.

"That's what people were talking about," Sandy recalled.

Purcell Powless was not the person to comment on the issue he had worked hard to support. Tribal spokesman Rick Wheelock, *Kalihwisaks* editor at the time, issued a press statement about the court update. He said the tribe conducts bingo pursuant to a tribal ordinance adopted by the tribe and that games are conducted solely by tribal members on tribal property. Proceeds help provide health and education services to tribal elders and youth, he said.

The disputed election did not result in a recount, however. The *Kalihwisaks* reported that some factions claimed ineligible voters had cast ballots; others claimed a conflict of interest existed because two of Purcell's family members were on the Election Board that handled recounts. At a General Tribal Council meeting August 15, the members approved a motion to adopt the original election results. The meeting was held in a science classroom at the Sacred Heart Center. There were few chairs. Most people stood. A vote was taken by show of hands.

Gary Metoxen was sworn in as the new tribal chairman. Purcell accepted the decision. He had kept up on his union dues over the years.

Purcell called the ironworkers' union to look for work again in construction.

Notes

1. Letter from Bingo Committee Secretary Lillian King to parking attendant Fredmond "Fritz" Hill, February 28, 1980. Bingo Committee records.

2. Peter Naze, affidavit, case file of *Oneida Tribe v. Brown County Sheriff Norb Froelich*, US District Court, Western District of Wisconsin, 81C54.

3. "Bingo on Indian Land May Become Legal Fight," *Green Bay Press-Gazette*, February 3, 1980.

4. *Seminole Tribe of Florida v. Robert Butterworth* (491 F. Supp. 1015, Dist. Co. SD Florida 1980).

5. Gerald L. Hill, Oneida Elder Interview with L. Gordon McLester III, Oneida Cultural Heritage Department, 1998.

6. Ambrose I. Lane Sr., *Return of the Buffalo: The Story Behind America's Indian Gaming Explosion* (Westport, CT: Bergin & Garvey, 1995).

7. Peter Naze worked as an assistant district attorney in Brown County from 1972 to 1975, then was in private practice before serving as district attorney from 1977 to 1987. He was elected Brown County circuit court judge and served twenty years on the bench before retiring in 2008. He died in 2009 at age sixty-six.

8. The Menominee is the only tribe exempted from Public Law 280 in Wisconsin.

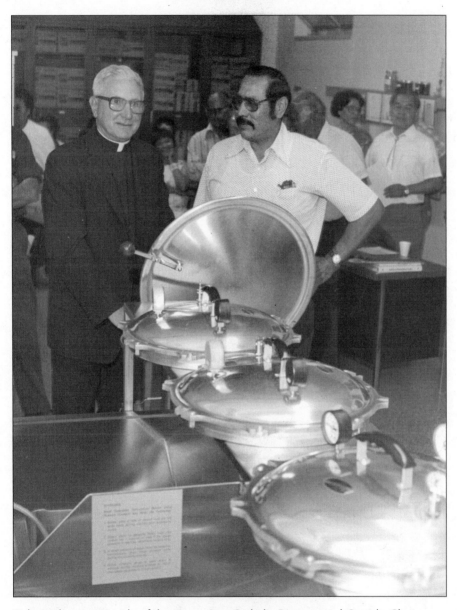

Bishop Aloysius Wycislo of the Green Bay Catholic Diocese and Oneida Chairman
Purcell Powless were on hand for the dedication of the tribal cannery at the dio-
cese's Sacred Heart Center on July 14, 1978. *Press-Gazette Collection of the Neville
Public Museum of Brown County*

Shirley and Al Czech of Green Bay. Shirley remains a loyal bingo player. *Courtesy of Shirley Czech*

Bingo players Harold "Whitey" and Audrey Klika of Green Bay. Whitey ran the Bay theater in Green Bay. *Courtesy of Judy Sustman*

Drummers riding in the back of a pickup were part of the annual parade to kick off the Oneida powwow in 1979. *Kalihwisaks Collection, Oneida Tribe of Indians*

Couples dance during the annual Oneida powwow in 1979. *Press-Gazette Collection of the Neville Public Museum of Brown Co.*

A bingo player at the civic center buys cards in this undated photo.
Kalihwisaks Collection, Oneida Tribe of Indians

Purcell Powless chaired the Oneida tribe nearly continuously from 1967 to 1990.
Kalihwisaks Collection, Oneida Tribe of Indians

From left, attorney Gerald L. Hill, Amos Christjohn, and Ernie L. Stevens Jr. talk in
the parking lot at Sacred Heart Center in about 1979. Ernest Jr., wearing a Soaring
Eagles boxing club jacket, said he counted Jerry and his grand-uncle Amos as two
of his mentors. *Kalihwisaks Collection, Oneida Tribe of Indians*

The Irene Moore Activity Center opened April 9, 1983, on Airport Drive as the new and current home of Oneida Bingo. *Kalihwisaks Collection, Oneida Tribe of Indians*

The bingo floor at the IMAC, shown in about 1985, was expanded to accommodate up to 1,200 players. *Kalihwisaks Collection, Oneida Tribe of Indians*

Bingo managers Sandra Ninham, left, and Alma Webster beneath a portrait of Irene Moore in about 1983. *Kalihwisaks Collection, Oneida Tribe of Indians*

Attorney Gerald L. Hill   Ernest L. Stevens Jr.
Oneida Tribe of Indians   *Oneida Tribe of Indians*

Attorney Francis Skenandore
Oneida Tribe of Indians

Attorney Sharon (House) Cornelius
Oneida Tribe of Indians

Governor Anthony Earl called bingo during a visit to the Irene Moore Activity Center on January 10, 1986, substituting briefly for caller Jennifer McLester, left, as bingo manager Sandy Ninham looked on. *Reprinted by permission, Green Bay Press-Gazette*

Governor Tommy Thompson joked with tribal members as he played bingo during a visit to the Oneida Indian Reservation on May 18, 1987. Surrounding Thompson, from left, were Purcell Powless, George Reed, Sandy Ninham, and Alma Webster.
Reprinted by permission, Green Bay Press-Gazette

Oneida elder Samantha Farmer, left, and Oneida Cannery
supervisor Vickie Cornelius dry white corn in the cannery in
about 1992. *Kalihwisaks Collection, Oneida Tribe of Indians*

A ribbon-cutting ceremony was held in July 1992 for a branch casino prior to
the main Oneida Casino's opening in 1993. Those on hand included, from left,
Amos Christjohn, Debbie Doxtator, Kathy Hughes, Louise Cornelius, Lois Strong,
Don Denny, Artley Skenandore Jr., Keller Inc. project manager Larry Anderson,
and Ernest Stevens Sr. *Kalihwisaks Collection, Oneida Tribe of Indians*

Menominee activist Ada Deer, left, with Oneida chairwoman Debbie (Skenandore) Doxtator in about 1993. *Kalihwisaks Collection, Oneida Tribe of Indians*

Three women again after three decades: Sandy (Ninham) Brehmer, left, and Alma Webster are shown in May 2013 beneath the portrait of Irene Moore, which hangs in the Irene Moore Activity Center. *Dennis King/DKingofimagez.com*

CHAPTER 7

Acculturation: American-izing and Oneida-cizing

*I look at bingo as the first step in our funding. . . .
Bingo was like a big corn crop. It was a transition
to another whole era.* —Dr. Carol Cornelius,
Oneida Cultural Heritage Department

I READ through about ten years of *Kalihwisaks* issues during several weeks of visits to the Oneida Cultural Heritage Department. Then I interviewed Carol Cornelius, the director of Cultural Heritage at the time. Most people call her Dr. Carol, just as her car's Oneida license plate said. (Her next plate said AKHSOT, meaning "grandmother.") Dr. Carol grew up near Shawano in the 1950s and regularly came to see family in Oneida.

"I used to come visit my great-grandmother Sophie Cornelius on Tip Road. It was a big deal to drive here, a big adventure. There were nine of us in a car. It was horrendous. I remember she had a long, rutted driveway. They all spoke Oneida, my great-grandma and her daughters. They shooed us kids outside while they talked. But we were around it. That's something we're revitalizing today."

Dr. Carol studied at the University of Wisconsin–Green Bay, UW–Madison, and State University of New York–Fredonia. She received her doctorate in 1992 from Cornell University and has authored two books.

I asked her about gaming's impact on the tribe and her department.

"I was out East going to school in 1976 when bingo started," Dr. Carol said. "I heard a story about a lady who made homemade buns for hamburgers. When bingo started at the civic center, she made a few dozen for the players. She quickly ran out and had to make more and more. Pretty soon that's all she was doing. I thought that was an amazing story."

Back then, the tribe did not have a cultural heritage department, she told me. The Oneida Nation Museum started in 1979 with grant funding. Cultural Heritage evolved out of the museum's mission and became its own department in 1995. The Oneida Nation funds the Oneida Cultural Heritage Department largely from gaming and tobacco revenue. The department also receives some grants.

"The greatest impact is being able to fund the language program," Dr. Carol said. There were eleven people who spoke Oneida as a first language when classes began. When I interviewed her in 2010, Dr. Carol said there were only two first-language speakers alive as teachers.[1] About a dozen younger people now have learned to speak Oneida, although they are not quite fluent.

"It's just amazing we're able to do this," she said.

"I always look at bingo as the first step in our funding. Bingo was a big start to having some programs and services for our people. It's fantastic that women were saying we can raise our own funds. Even before bingo, our elders used to have fund-raisers. Women would hold a spaghetti dinner, kind of like a community ethos or ethics," she said.

Acculturation—the process of adapting to a new or different culture—can work both ways. There can be mutual influence of different cultures in close contact. The Oneida adapted to the dominant culture while retaining their traditional ethos. In forging a national identity, Americans cast off European class structure and customs that no longer fit. Americans learned from natives to grow corn, potatoes, and tobacco and perhaps acquired a taste for freedom, gender equality, and democracy from indigenous people as well.

The Oneida are one of six nations of the Haudenosaunee, or what Europeans called the Iroquois Confederacy. The Iroquois were among the first tribes to have contact with European immigrants and have been the subject of much study. Books on the Haudenosaunee often refer to them as a matriarchal or matrilineal society.

"*Matriarchal* means power. *Matrilineal* means descent through the mother," Dr. Carol noted. "Women gathered the corn. Men hunted. This was serious business, these roles. Women were bringing in the food. I think that still plays today. The women make sure everyone is taken care of. My auntie, Great-Aunt Helen Skenandore, talked about mutual aid societies. If someone's house burned down, the women made sure people got together to build a new one. The men rebuilt it and the women cooked a meal to feed all the men who showed up to work. They would harvest corn with help from the men and then have a meal. I look at bingo as the same thing. We were able to provide that meal. Bingo was like a big corn crop. It was a transition to another whole era." Bingo revenue represented a new crop for the tribe. "It helped sustain us," she said.

Women have maintained the role of providers in the community, Dr. Carol argues. "I think that's something we've always done and are expected to do," she said. "The same thing with churches and clans: women get together and get it done. It's what you do if someone needs help."

It's important for Oneida people to know their clans, Dr. Carol added. "Because during midwinter ceremonies, that's when babies got their names. So you must know your clan," she said. "More people are getting their names now as adults. Because of our history and everything that's happened to us, many people didn't have the opportunity. They weren't doing it. That's something we're revitalizing. They say when you go to the Creator's world, you will be recognized by your Oneida name. So you need to have it. It's part of your identity. Language is what makes us unique people in the world. There are only so many Oneidas in the whole world. It's our language; it's what the Creator gave us. I tell people it's our birthright, to speak our own language. If we were supposed to speak French, we would have been born in France. But we were born here. We're Oneida so we should speak Oneida and keep it alive."

The interview with Dr. Carol set me on a hunt to learn more about the traditional role of Haudenosaunee women. A crop of corn, I soon learned, was more than a metaphor for a bingo game. The power of women and the role of corn were intertwined in a complex kinship system in Haudenosaunee culture.

I found one of Dr. Carol's books at the Oneida Library, located in the Oscar Archiquette building in Site I. In her book *Iroquois Corn in a Culture-Based Curriculum: A Framework for Respectfully Teaching About Cultures*, Dr. Carol argued that corn is dependent on humans and humans are dependent on corn in a reciprocal relationship. "Corn is truly a gift to the world from the people of the western hemisphere. It became an important U.S. crop and affected the world economy," she wrote. Corn influenced Haudenosaunee values, beliefs, economy, and even type of housing.

Chaz Wheelock loaned me a book by Jane Mt. Pleasant, associate professor of horticulture and former director of the American Indian Program at Cornell University. In *Traditional Iroquois Corn: Its History, Cultivation and Use*, the author says corn, more than any other aspect of Iroquois life, reflects the persistence of Iroquois people, the complexity of their cultural institutions, and their contributions to life. Corn plays recurring roles in key oral texts, including the creation story of life beginning on Turtle Island; the Great Law of Peace, which describes Haudenosaunee governance; the Code of Handsome Lake; and the Thanksgiving Address, which describes the Haudenosaunee worldview.

Throughout Iroquois history, women have been intimately linked to corn, Mt. Pleasant wrote. They were entrusted with its care and were dependent on corn as sustainers of life. Women are able to coax life from Mother Earth. In the Iroquois creation story, corn (along with tobacco) was one of the plants that sprouted from the grave of Skywoman's daughter, the first mother born on Earth.[2]

Women and corn played key roles as the Iroquois Confederacy was established. Iroquoia, the area dominated by Iroquois culture, was in a state of near-constant warfare in rounds of attacks and retaliation. The Peacemaker, a Huron from the north side of Lake Ontario, arrived in Iroquoia to propose a new governance system based on the ritual of condolence and community representation and participation in a central council. The women had enabled the warriors to make war by providing them with food. The Peacemaker met with Jigonsaseh, a powerful corn grower from the West, and asked that the women stop feeding the warriors. Jigonsaseh agreed but negotiated a powerful role for women in the confederacy: clan mothers would appoint and depose the chiefs who represented the clans and nations in central council. A chief wore deer antlers as a symbol of his authority. If he failed as a leader, clan mothers were empowered to remove his antlers.[3]

The Thanksgiving Address is recited in Haudenosaunee communities to remind people of the essentials of life, according to Mt. Pleasant. It expresses a sense of connection, a relationship with earth and with nature. Corn is meant to be raised by extended families and shared as a community.

It is a gift from the Creator. All parts of the universe are related as members of an extended family. Corn, beans, and squash, known as the Three Sisters, share a unique relationship. They provide food for the Iroquois, who in turn give thanks, respect, and care to the plants. The Three Sisters are viewed as female members of the extended human family.

No plant was more vitally important in the New World's history than Indian corn or maize. The name comes from the Arawak word *mahiz*. Christopher Columbus first mentioned the plant being cultivated on the island of Haiti. Indians provided corn to settlers at Plymouth and Jamestown, helping rescue them from starvation.

Corn is believed to have evolved from teosinte, a grass found in the central highlands of Mexico and Guatemala. Indigenous farmers began breeding this wild ancestor of corn six thousand years ago. Over several millennia, corn was transported north and south from Central America and became the main food staple of many indigenous peoples. It became the economic foundation of Iroquois people. Cooking corn with wood ash is known as alkaline cooking.[4]

Eating corn and beans together provides a complete protein for the human diet. Squash adds carbohydrates and sugars. The Haudenosaunee people grew the Three Sisters together in a mound so that each sister supported the other. Scientists call it companion planting. Each sister had unique characteristics that benefited the others. The cornstalks support the beans to climb, the beans add nitrogen to the soil, and broad squash leaves keep moisture in the mounds and provide ground cover to keep down weeds.

Corn was braided into long strings and placed in rafters of the longhouse to dry. The braids hung like garland throughout the longhouse. Nothing of the corn plant went to waste. Corn husks were made into mats, footwear, and dolls. Dr. Carol's book *Iroquois Corn in a Culture-Based Curriculum* contains an interview with Katsi Cook, an Akwesasne Mohawk midwife. Dr. Carol talked with Katsi (pronounced Gah-jee) about an article for young people called "Corn in My Kitchen."

"I never really understood the corn until I started growing it and looking for the metaphors and analogies in the culture," Katsi told her. "I guess as a midwife, I really never had the depth of understanding before about traditional roles of Iroquois women until I grew corn. I know John Mohawk used to say that the power of the Iroquois women came through their control of agriculture. Fields came under the domain of women. He said women controlled the sexual economy of the village because they decided who would mate, who the couples would be that produced children. . . . The notion of corn in my kitchen is really a wonderful one because it brings home to us something that is very complex and in every part of our lives, our spiritual lives, even our emotional lives. The relationships between the corn, beans, and squash, the Three Sisters, the companionship, again, a nurturing relationship, is what helps the corn to grow."[5]

Katsi said people in Mexico believe that when corn is hanging in your kitchen drying it's the same as when there's a baby in the house. "You have to talk nice to each other. You have to be respectful of one another. You can't use any angry language or bad words because the corn can hear you. If it hears all this negativity, it won't grow for you next year. It teaches us to take care of each other. We need to protect the earth," she said. "I think corn is the best teacher. Working in gardens is almost like having a college out here."[6]

Iroquois women not only were farmers and cooks but also played an important political role because of their power to name and remove confederacy chiefs. Arthur C. Parker wrote about Haudenosaunee women in his book *Parker on the Iroquois.* Arthur was the grandnephew of Ely Parker, a Seneca who served in the Union army under Gen. Ulysses S. Grant. In 1851 Ely had collaborated with Lewis Henry Morgan to write *League of the Haudenosaunee, or Iroquois,* which chronicled female Iroquois influence.

Arthur C. Parker carried on the tradition in 1968 when he wrote that civil chiefs were nominated by certain noble women in whose families the titles were hereditary; the nominations were confirmed by popular councils both of men and of women and finally by the confederate council.

"Women thus had great power for not only could they nominate their rulers but also depose them for incompetency in office. Here, then, we find the right of popular nomination, the right of recall and of woman suffrage, all flourishing in the old America of the Red Man and centuries before it became the clamor of the new America of the white invader. Who now shall call Indians and Iroquois savages!"[7] The right of American women to vote was not recognized until 1920.

The Iroquois divided labors by gender, Parker continued. The function of the men was to hunt, bring in game, defend their homes and property, and engage in war expeditions. The women were in charge of the crops. The women of each settlement each year elected a chief matron to direct their work in the communal fields. The chief matron ordered all the details of planting, cultivation, and harvesting. Most cornfields were owned by the tribe or clan. Individuals might cultivate their own fields if they were willing to do their share in the tribal fields. If they did not do this they could not claim their share of the communal harvest. The women of a community who own individual fields may work together with their husbands and male friends to form a mutual aid society (known as "in the good rule as they assist one another"), to help with corn planting. It is the duty of the owner of the field to provide a feast at the end of the hoeing bee, and each helper takes home her supply of corn soup, hominy, or bread. After the hoeing and before eating, the women flock to the nearest stream or pond to bathe. There is much singing, laughing, and joking. In the autumn, the communal harvesting begins. It was not uncommon for men to join in the husking bee. The men were called by the women to help.[8]

"They were lured to the scene by the promise of soup, song and the society of wise old matrons and shy maidens," Parker wrote. "The older women carefully noted the industry of their younger assistants, and scheming parents were able to obtain information about prospective mates for their children."

The Iroquois were not great eaters, meaning they seldom gorged themselves with food at meals or feasts. To do so ordinarily would be a religious offense and destroy the capacity to withstand hunger. Children were trained to eat frugally and taught that overeating was far worse than undereating. The large appetites of white men who visited them were often a matter of surprise to the Indians who entertained them.[9]

Even though women had great authority, they did not dominate or rule. Women were respected for their wisdom and for being keepers of the culture. Gretchen L. Green, as an assistant professor of history at Rockhurst College in Kansas City, Missouri, wrote about native women and colonial acculturation. In an essay, she said that Native American feminism today is concerned with restoring the gender balance of power lost when European customs and values encroached on native ones. The balance of male and female roles and their interdependence were socially, culturally, economically, and politically necessary. Separate gender roles did not mean

gender inequity, Green wrote. Women had their own rights and responsibilities and were in no way secondary to the men. Iroquois women held
such power because of their gender, not in spite of it.[10]

Historians suggest that the Iroquois system of government influenced
the American concept of democracy with separate branches of government
serving as checks and balances. Benjamin Franklin looked to the Iroquois
for ideas that would break with the European tradition of concentrating
power in the hands of a monarch. Sally Roesch Wagner is a member of the
National Organization for Women and the executive director of the Matilda
Joslyn Gage Foundation in Fayetteville, New York. She said that not only
did the Iroquois influence American government, but the role of Iroquois
women helped inspire nineteenth-century feminists in their call for reform.
When activist Lucretia Mott and her husband visited the Seneca in 1848,
she saw that Iroquois women had equal responsibility in government, economic, family, and spiritual matters. Afterward she visited friends who organized the first women's rights convention in Seneca Falls, New York, in
1848.

Wagner said Matilda Joslyn Gage, a feminist of that era, believed that
the US form of government was borrowed from that of the Six Nations, and
thus "the modern world [is] indebted [to the Iroquois] for its first conception
of inherent rights, natural equality of condition, and the establishment of a
civilized government upon this basis."[11]

The role of Iroquois women may have been envied by reformers of the
era, but their lives were nonetheless harsh and dominated by bloodshed.
War remained a constant threat. The Haudenosaunee were unified in peace
among themselves and remained a formidable force against enemy native nations. To protect their borders, plunder furs, and take captives, the
Haudenosaunee launched frequent raids against tribes and crushed the
Huron, Petun, Algonquin, Neutral, and Erie tribes and forced the Susque-
hannock to relocate.

At a societal level, warfare and the taking of war prisoners also helped
the Haudenosaunee deal with deaths in their ranks due to war and disease.
Warriors often took captives from other tribes to replace their numbers
killed in raids. Captives were either killed or adopted. The Oneida, who had
suffered devastating losses in raids and whose population was decimated
by the 1750s, relied especially on adopting outsiders. Some adoptees were
"requickened" in the name and role of a deceased family member.[12]

Haudenosaunee women of the mourning household could demand a new raid to obtain more captives. The target of a mourning-war campaign was usually an enemy tribe. When the victors returned home, village leaders apportioned captives to the grieving lineages, whose elder women then chose to adopt or execute them. Deaths of warriors in these raids prompted more grieving, which led to a new call for more raids in a never-ending cycle of war.[13]

Haudenosaunee leaders developed diplomatic skills to maintain their neutrality toward the Dutch, French, and English powers. Treaty making and the use of oratory extended the Great Peace to a broader stage. The Haudenosaunee considered themselves not subjects but allies of the British Crown, each nation of the alliance with a hand on the covenant chain. Treaty making served to polish the chain and keep it from rusting.

The Haudenosaunee recorded the symbolism of the covenant chain in the Two Row Wampum treaty, an agreement with the Dutch that was extended to the British and later the Americans.[14] The wampum belt consists of two rows of purple beads made from quahog shells set against a background of white beads. The purple beads represent two vessels—a Haudenosaunee canoe and a European ship—traveling together down the river of life; they are parallel but not touching. To the Haudenosaunee, the relationship is that of brothers, not father and son. Neither person will interfere with the other's internal affairs. Neither will get into the other's boat. Neither will try to steer the other's vessel.

The Haudenosaunee alliance shattered in 1776 when the Six Nations split and chose sides between the English Crown and the American colonists. Polly Cooper's sharing of Oneida corn with starving American troops wintering at Valley Forge in 1777–1778 resonated with symbolic significance, recalling the political deal struck by the legendary Jigonsaseh. The British and their Indian allies, some of them Iroquois, targeted Oneida and Tuscarora villages for destruction. The Colonial army, in turn, targeted the food crops of the four Iroquois tribes that sided with the British.

"The Indians shall see that there is malice enough in our hearts to destroy everything that contributes to their support," Maj. Gen. John Sullivan said in his report to Congress about the 1779 Iroquois raids.

The burning of corn crops, however, was a greater blow than destruction of their towns. The Genesee Valley, the fertile garden region of the Seneca, was cultivated for miles. Sullivan destroyed forty towns, obliterated sixty thousand bushels of corn, and uprooted fruit orchards, one containing fifteen hundred trees, according to his report.

, After the revolution, the Haudenosaunee lost vast pieces of hunting lands. The loss spelled an end to large hunting expeditions, effectively ending the men's role as hunter-providers and rendering them jobless.

Amid this climate in 1799 an influential religious leader emerged among the Haudenosaunee. A Seneca man named Handsome Lake, born in 1735 on the Genesee River near Avon, New York, suffered as an alcoholic and was an invalid for years. He claimed he had visions revealing the will of the Creator. His visions developed into a religion that revitalized Iroquois culture by urging sobriety, morality, and native self-sufficiency. Handsome Lake's religion blended traditional native rituals with certain innovations. He took his message to other Iroquois nations. He urged children to attend school and learn to use American tools. He urged Iroquois men to farm as white people did, and not think of farming as women's work.

According to Parker, Handsome Lake's message afforded hope, by preserving Iroquois identity while adapting to a new future. The Iroquois selectively adopted new ideas that best fit traditional customs.

"That's something our people have done. I would call it a survival technique," Dr. Carol told me in our interview. "In the onslaught of new stuff coming at us, how were we going to survive? The Code of Handsome Lake was all about that. In 1799 our world was totally tipped upside down. How are we going to live? What values stay? What do we do? He had that vision about what we should be doing," she said. The idea was to adapt and reinforce traditional culture while living in a new world.

Syncretism is a Greek word that means "facilitating coexistence and unity between otherwise different cultures and contradictory worldviews." Plutarch wrote that the Cretans compromised and reconciled their differences and came together in alliance when faced with external dangers. In religious syncretism, for example, Germanic and Celtic pagan views were incorporated into Christianity.

Syncretism can be used to describe how the Oneidas accepted the Christian church while still holding onto their traditional customs, Dr. Carol said.

Haudenosaunee clothing evolved into a mix of calico trade cloth and traditional beads and ribbons. At powwows today, Iroquois women can be seen wearing beaded caps based on the style of Glengarry military caps worn by British regiments in Canada. The caps were popular Hudson Bay Co. trade items with Indians.

"Another way to look at it is that when we see something, we Oneida-cize it," she said. "You give us tennis shoes, we're going to put beads on it. Give us T-shirts or hoodies, we put our designs on it. Well, that's what our people did with the church, because the hymns are in Oneida. So they keep a big part of who they are along with the new belief system."

The Oneida Hymn Singers of Wisconsin, a group honored by the National Endowment for the Arts in 2008 for their cultural contributions, has been singing Christian hymns in the Oneida language for nearly one hundred years. Brian Doxtator, a member of the group and an Oneida storyteller, told me there was another motive at work among hymn singers. While the obvious mission was to help bring Christianity to those who spoke only Oneida, the hymn singers also were preserving Oneida voices at a time when assimilationist America was trying to silence the language, he said. The group has succeeded in keeping the Oneida language alive in song.

"That syncretism is the blending," Dr. Carol told me. "They do that in order to survive. There are contradictory elements. People are always struggling to make it fit. We blended it all together so it's acceptable."

Notes

1. Leona (Doxtator) Smith died at age ninety-one in 2011. Maria (Christ-john) Hinton died at age 103 in 2013. The efforts of language revitalization trace back to the WPA project directed by Professor Floyd Lounsbury. Several dozen Oneida speakers helped teach the language. Professor Cliff Abbott of the University of Wisconsin–Green Bay continued Lounsbury's efforts. Abbott has worked with the Oneida since 1974 to preserve and teach the language. Abbott, Maria Hinton, and Amos Christjohn compiled "An Oneida Dictionary" in 1996. It is now available online at www.uwgb.edu/oneida.

2. "The Creation Story," www.oneidanation.org/culture.

3. Jane Mt. Pleasant, *Traditional Iroquois Corn: Its History, Cultivation and Use* (Ithaca, NY: Northeast Regional, 2011).

4. Ibid.

5. Carol Cornelius, *Iroquois Corn in a Culture-Based Curriculum: A Framework for Respectfully Teaching About Cultures* (Albany: State University of New York, 1999).

6. Ibid.

7. Arthur C. Parker, *Parker on the Iroquois* (New York: Syracuse University Press, 1968).

8. Ibid.

9. Ibid.

10. Gretchen L. Green, "Gender and the Longhouse: Iroquois Women in a Changing Culture," in *Women and Freedom in Early America*, edited by Larry Eldridge (New York: New York University Press, 1997), pp. 7–25.

11. Sally Roesch Wagner, *Sisters in Spirit: Haudenosaunee (Iroquois) Influence on Early American Feminists* (Summertown, TN: Native Voices, 2001).

12. Daniel K. Richter, *The Ordeal of the Longhouse* (Chapel Hill: University of North Carolina Press, 1992).

13. Ibid.

14. The four hundredth anniversary of the Two Row Wampum treaty was celebrated in 2013. The Five Nations made the agreement with Dutch representatives in 1613. The Haudenosaunee consider it the basis for subsequent treaties, including the Covenant Chain treaty with England in 1677 and Treaty of Canandaigua with the United States in 1794.

CHAPTER 8

The House That Women Built

*They took our land and gave us the Bible. Now they
have the land and we have the church's most sacred
institution . . . Bingo.* —Comedian Charlie Hill[1]

WITH AN encouraging court ruling on bingo in the summer of 1981, the
Oneida hoped to build on their success and move out of the cramped gymnasium. The ruling came on the heels of an election for new leadership.
Gary Metoxen was sworn in as chairman, having defeated Purcell Powless by three votes on July 25. Judge Barbara Crabb, on July 27, denied the
state's motion to dismiss Oneida's suit over bingo. The case wasn't over,
however, and still could go to trial. The judge's reasoning that civil regulatory issues such as bingo were within tribal jurisdiction gave the Oneida
hope. At a special meeting October 20, 1981, the Business Committee, under
chairman Metoxen, discussed amending the bingo ordinance to raise prize
totals from two thousand dollars to three thousand dollars during a single
bingo session.

After Judge Crabb issued the 1981 ruling, tribal attorneys asked for a
permanent injunction to specify the state had no jurisdiction on tribal
bingo. A pretrial conference was held April 6, 1982, in federal court in Madison. Francis Skenandore and Milt Rosenberg appeared for the tribe. John
Niemisto appeared for the state. US Magistrate William Gansner said Judge
Crabb's opinion and order had resolved most of the legal questions. The
parties stipulated to the facts and the court decided summary judgment in
favor of the tribe on May 28, 1982, permanently enjoining the state and local
law enforcement from interfering with bingo on the reservation.[2]

"It is clearly a victory for the tribe," Metoxen told the *Green Bay Press-
Gazette.* The story also quoted tribal attorney Francis Skenandore as saying

the ruling verified that the tribe has a right to self-government and a right to make its own laws.[3]

The Oneida case did not serve as a legal precedent, yet it had enormous impact. Other tribes in the region opened their own bingo halls and some contacted Oneida for advice. The Oneida hosted bingo seminars for native nations interested in starting operations.

"After the lawsuit, we were in the public eye," Sandy Ninham said. "People either came to us or we went to them." One of the first visits the Oneida made was to the Forest County Potawatomi in Crandon, Wisconsin, which held bingo in a small gym. The Oneida later met with tribal leaders from Stockbridge-Munsee, Lac Courte Oreilles, and Lac du Flambeau in Wisconsin. At these seminars, Sandy, Alma Webster, Pat Misikin, and Kathy Hughes usually offered suggestions, Jerry Hill described legal aspects, and Mark Powless discussed government concerns for bingo.

Soon, bingo would be humming on the "moccasin telegraph" to other tribes around the country.

Franklin Ducheneaux, a member of the Cheyenne River Sioux Tribe of South Dakota and counsel to the House Interior Committee for eighteen years, recalled going to conferences in the early 1980s and meeting tribal colleagues who'd say, "Well, we're doing a little bingo, making a little money."

"'Oh, are you really? Well, maybe we'll do that.' And they would go back home and start things up . . . just basic bingo, not very high stakes. It was just to raise a little money for a fire department or a Head Start program, and so on."[4]

More than eighty tribes across the country soon looked to gaming as a way to raise revenue. Some tribes opened card rooms offering poker and blackjack, but most gaming at this time consisted of bingo. Even without slot machines or casino-style games, the Indian gaming industry grew rapidly in the early 1980s. Some of these tribes, too, found themselves in litigation over gaming. In San Diego County, for example, the Barona Group of the Capitan Grande Band of Mission Indians sued in federal court after the local sheriff threatened to shut down its bingo operations. The Barona won.

The Florida Seminole case allowing bingo was affirmed by the Fifth Circuit US Court of Appeals, and the Supreme Court declined to review the case. The Cabazon-Morongo case would take several more years to move through the courts.

Jerry Hill said some tribes were going further than the Oneida and wanted to put in slot machines. "We said that wasn't part of the issue. We kept it confined to bingo. Our argument was based on the formulation of state law at the time, which defined bingo as a regulated activity. We wanted to keep it at that, because if we got off into casino gambling, those were defined as crimes. And we didn't want that argument. So it was kind of a careful strategy," he said.

The bingo stalemate had been resolved, but the Oneida remained in conflict with the state over the sale of untaxed cigarettes on the reservation. On January 27, 1982, police raided an Oneida tobacco outlet and arrested a tribal employee, Ida Stevens, for possessing untaxed cigarettes. In October 1982, individual Oneida sought licenses from the tribe to sell cigarettes in their businesses, according to the *Kalihwisaks*. At issue was whether retail tobacco would be a tribal enterprise or a franchise granted to individual tribal members. Some tribal members wanted to sell tobacco on their own through individual franchises. Jerry Hill felt that was the wrong approach.

"Bingo was based on the fact we could regulate it ourselves and that's what we were protecting," Jerry said. "So if the ordinance needed changing, the council could change it. It was the tribe's monopoly, just as we did with cigarettes. The tribe would do it and no other tribal member could do it individually."

But some questioned Jerry's stance and that of the tribal leadership. Critics said the centralized policy deterred innovation and discouraged independent small businesses run by tribal members. Jerry maintained that individual tobacco franchises would have become an independent, unregulated activity. "That isn't what we wanted. What we wanted to say is that this is completely regulated by the tribe, for the tribe, for the benefit of the tribe," he said.

In April 1982, the *Kalihwisaks* reported the governor vetoed a bill to impose a tax on tribal tobacco sales. The story credited Mary Greendeer, an Oneida tribal member on the governor's Domestic Abuse Committee, with helping facilitate a resolution to resolve the tobacco issue. The 1983 agreement between the state and tribe rebated 70 percent of Wisconsin cigarette taxes to the tribe.

"We had just gotten done fighting the cigarette wars. We won that mainly not by beating the state so much as holding the state to a limitation by agreeing to a formula for rebating that part of the tobacco sales that went to tribal members," Jerry said.

Bingo and tobacco were examples of business forays that Indian tribes began pursuing under court rulings evolving in the late 1970s and early 1980s. After the court ruling on bingo, Oneida Bingo needed to improve its accounting system to deal with the steady increase of cash flow. "There was just a whole bunch of money. Rumors and suspicions circulated about people stealing money from the tribe. You couldn't buy a new car without starting rumors you were stealing from the tribe," said attorney Jerry Hill. When bingo got big, money was not accounted for properly. That was one of the issues scrutinized by tribal managers and the beginning of better accountability.

Out went the cigar-box cash register and lumber company aprons for handling money. The managers implemented better internal control standards to minimize the chance of theft and collusion by employees or players.

"Gary Metoxen at one point wanted bingo workers to wear jumpsuits with tight-fitting wristbands so that employees couldn't shove money up their sleeves," Sandy said. According to Jerry, Gary also wanted an outside management firm to come in and run the Oneida operation.

"Francis and I argued we needed to do it ourselves," Jerry said. It was part of growing pains. The tribe trained its own workforce to do the job. By that time, the tribe had about ten years of middle-management experience.

The Oneida Bingo Committee in turn visited the Florida Seminoles to learn about their high-stakes bingo operation. At its meeting March 20, 1982, the committee had discussed traveling to Florida to see how the Seminoles operated bingo "to bring home new ideas to improve our bingo." Secretary Lillian King's notes recorded the questions they wanted answered: "what type of supplies they use, how they handle their money, how they pay out cash prizes, what kind of bookkeeping they do, how they control their cards, what kind of storage they have and how to improve profits in our kitchen."

The Oneida also recognized they needed to work with other tribes on common interests in gaming. Mark Powless, the young tribal councilman who had accompanied the women managers on their first trip to buy bingo supplies in Chicago in 1976, later headed the National Indian Gaming Task Force. The group existed from 1983 to 1988 and was meant to be a clearinghouse of information for tribes interested in pursuing gaming. The National Indian Gaming Association (NIGA) was created in 1985 to represent gaming tribes, partly as a result of task force recommendations. NIGA's mission was to advance the general welfare and self-sufficiency of Indian people through gaming enterprises. Purcell Powless would be its first vice chairman.

The Oneida had a common interest in the ability and intent to self-regulate gaming, Jerry said.

The tribe also was moving ahead on a new site for bingo. Oneida Bingo "has a very loyal following. But as pots grow larger, we have to turn away people," said Bruce King, a tribal economic development specialist, in a 1982 memo outlining the problems with the current location. Despite a lack of advertising of the events, bingo players came from as far away as Chicago and Crystal Falls, Michigan, the memo said. In 1982, the average session grossed $7,796. The first game in 1976 grossed $85. The civic center had just two small men's and women's bathrooms. A lagoon sanitary system at Site I was not able to adequately treat sewage generated with bingo four days a week. A new location would fit with the tribe's goals for safety and welfare of the bingo workers, including the bingo ladies, said the memo by Bruce King, a son of Lillian and Edwin King. Based on his research, he recommended as a new bingo location first the airport site, second the seminary property, third the industrial park off West Mason Street and fourth the Summers tract west of Northeast Wisconsin Technical College.

At a June 1982 meeting, the Bingo Committee discussed adding internal control procedures at the new bingo building without losing the "friendly, family atmosphere, holiday specials and giveaways" players expected. Planners envisioned using the center as a multiuse facility that could accommodate General Tribal Council meetings as well as bingo. Bingo Committee chair Sandra Ninham suggested naming the new building after Irene Moore in her memory, according to committee minutes.

On November 1, 1982, a groundbreaking ceremony was held for the new activity center across from the airport. The site was in a better commercial location, about three miles closer to Green Bay than the civic center. The twelve-thousand-square-foot building would accommodate six hundred players and have three hundred parking spots. It would be finished in March 1983. No federal money was used. That was significant in itself. The tribe took out a loan from the State Bank of De Pere for up to $450,000 to finance the new bingo facility.

That business transaction would have a big ripple effect, Kathy Hughes said. Hughes was on the Bingo Committee in 1982 along with Alma Webster, Lillian King, Kate Stevens, and Sandy Ninham.

"Our borrowing ability was so fragile then," Kathy said. The BIA guaranteed many tribal loans, but not for this venture. The loan was based on collateral income from bingo. From that relationship with the State Bank of De Pere, the Oneida tribe later bought $250,000 of the bank's stock. At the time, some tribal members called that move foolish, Kathy told me. But the stock split 4 to 1 a year later when the bank was acquired in a merger that became Associated Bank. The tribe's investment was then worth $1 million.

"That made an impression in the business community that we were moving," said Kathy, who had been the tribe's assistant controller in 1981. She later served terms as tribal vice chair and treasurer. She said profit wasn't really the goal when bingo started.

"From a gender perspective, women have different priorities than men. We were concerned with community, gathering people and keeping families together. Profit was really an after-effect," she said.

As planning for the new bingo building moved forward, the tribe became caught up once again in divisive politics. The Business Committee, under chairman Gary Metoxen, fired a tribal employee, Joe Villagomez, from his job as personnel manager. The firing sparked a storm of complaints. The *Kalihwisaks* reported that a GTC meeting on October 23, 1982, called for the removal of all Business Committee members for firing Villagomez. A special election of the Business Committee was set for December. In that election, Gary Metoxen was defeated. Purcell Powless, who had joined the race for his old job, was once again elected tribal chairman. He had been out of office sixteen months.

One of Purcell's first tasks as reelected chairman was dedicating the new bingo hall.

Bingo finally had a home of its own, one largely built by the efforts of women of the tribe. The Irene Moore Activity Center (IMAC) was dedicated April 9, 1983, at 2100 Airport Drive and was named in honor of the first woman elected chair of the Oneida Nation. Assisting Purcell at the ribbon cutting was Irene's widower, Simon Moore. At the dedication, family members described Irene as a tireless volunteer and organizer in the Oneida community. When asked by a newspaper in 1975 why she was involved in so many activities and projects, Irene had replied, "I just did things I thought had to be done."

"When politics entered into the community, women filled those jobs because we were the ones left home. Our men had to go off and get jobs, like Purcy, working the high rises," Sandy Ninham said.

In preparation for the opening of the new bingo hall, the Oneida tribe in March 1983 raised the total prize for a bingo session from three thousand dollars to twenty-five thousand dollars.

The first few bingo sessions at the new IMAC got off to a poor start, possibly because of bad weather or because players were not accustomed to the new location. Attendance fell to 250 during some early sessions. A few Oneida matrons, longtime players who had stakeholders' interest in the operation, met with bingo operators to talk about ways to get attendance up, recalled Loretta Webster, former tribal administrator and an early bingo volunteer. These veteran bingo players, sisters-in-law Lois and Angeline Powless, for example, offered advice on how to make the game better.

"They were also considered bingo queens," Elaine Skenandore told me. Tribal administrator Tony Utschig and bingo manager Sandy Ninham drew up a profit-and-loss analysis for sessions that drew as few as 200 people. A bingo session with 300 people breaks even; a session with 250 loses about eight hundred dollars and one of 200 people loses about eighteen hundred dollars, Tony said in a December 29, 1983, memo to the Business Committee. Tony and Sandy predicted that with a small crowd, bingo players would spend more than average because of the greatly increased chances of winning, especially when the announcers encouraged the situation. They found five sessions in December 1983 with attendance of 260 or fewer people. The low turnouts were blamed mostly on bad weather. Losses at the five sessions totaled five thousand dollars and were relatively small in relationship to gains. An average session at the time grossed $7,796. Bingo managers started announcing that they would continue to pay full prize money no matter how small the crowd. That encouraged the smaller crowds to buy more cards.

After bingo moved into the new building, players and employees saw changes immediately. Oneida Bingo increased its games from five sessions to eight sessions a week. Bingo personnel rose from thirty-three at the civic center to forty-eight at the IMAC, with openings to hire twelve more. Workers at the civic center were recruited from Site I residences or by friends at West De Pere schools. At the IMAC, workers came from all over the reservation. They filled out time cards and went on a payroll system that withheld income for taxes and Social Security. No more doling out pay in cash. Gone were the jeans and T-shirts for bingo employees. Workers now wore black pants and white shirts. It was a more professional operation.

Sandy Ninham was named bingo manager and Alma Webster assistant manager. Sandy received a $19,572 salary and Alma $18,160, according to a September 8, 1983, memo. The responsibilities of the two managers increased as well.

"What was once a part-time job has become a full-time career for both of us," Sandy said in the memo. They were in charge of everything at the new building: administrative record keeping, bank deposits, worker scheduling, inventory, supplies, kitchen, security, and maintenance.

Sandy had business cards made up for the two managers, but Alma wouldn't use hers. She didn't want a high-visibility role. So Sandy put Alma's name and title on her own business card, right under her name. That was fitting. They worked best as a team, each with a unique set of skills that contributed to the whole operation. Alma knew the numbers, and Sandy knew the people. Alma devised the games and decided the jackpots. Sandy was the mouthpiece for bingo. Her outgoing personality sold it to the crowd.

With bingo games expanded to eight times a week at the IMAC, attendance soon soared once again. Charter buses were bringing bingo players from across Wisconsin as well as Michigan's Upper Peninsula to play in Oneida. Within a year, crowds were so large that tribal leaders realized they had built too small. They needed to build an addition to accommodate six hundred more players.

"We had to turn down a couple of busloads of potential players and more than a dozen individuals," Sandy said. "People were driving in from two hundred miles or more only to be turned away because we just didn't have the room."

The expansion project in 1984 allowed the IMAC to accommodate up to twelve hundred players in a thirty-thousand-square-foot facility.

In 1984, the tribe completed its negotiations to buy the ninety-acre former seminary site, Sacred Heart Center, from the Green Bay Catholic

Diocese. The center replaced the sagging clapboard tribal building and former schoolhouse at Chicago Corners. On September 7, 1984, the tribe renamed it the Norbert Hill Center in honor of Norbert Hill Sr., who had served more than twenty years in tribal government. He had died June 19, 1983, at age seventy-one, while attending the annual banquet of the Detroit Indian Club, an organization he helped found thirty years earlier.

But the purchase of the Sacred Heart Center, now the Norbert Hill Center, was something of a gamble. Some tribal members thought the ninety-acre campus amounted to a white elephant that the tribe would never be able to fully utilize. It was too big and too expensive to maintain, some critics said.

The site in the 1890s had been the Oneida Boarding School, built by the government as an inducement to get Oneida people to accept allotment of the reservation. The boarding school closed in 1919 and the site was sold to non-Indians. The Green Bay Catholic Diocese bought the site in 1924 for a seminary, which closed in 1976. The diocese leased space to community groups and later put the property up for sale.

"We said we'd work out a payment plan. The proceeds of bingo allowed us to do that," Jerry Hill said. "The diocese had the site up for sale, but some Oneidas wanted us to interfere with any possible sale by threatening to cloud the title."

"We knew it would screw up the sale because nobody's going to buy property that's encumbered in a lawsuit," he said. "We did threaten a lawsuit. That parcel was never allotted, and our argument was that it reverted to the tribe when it was no longer used. The deal that was reached said we would pay eight hundred thousand dollars for improvements over five to seven years of a land contract. I don't know if people knew what a gamble it was because we had to scrounge up money for that land payment. The land was valued at $12 million. We got it for less than $1 million by paying for the improvements. Some tribal members asked why should we pay anything at all if it belonged to us. Francis [Skenandore] and I argued that if you want to do it that way we can fight it out in court but it may take twenty years and you may win. And in the meantime no one's using that building and it falls apart. So, do you want it now or later?"

The favorable bingo lawsuit decision, tobacco sales agreement, and acquisition of the former seminary campus were among early "quiet wins" for the tribe during a time of transformation, Jerry Hill said. The moves did not make big splashy news but helped build part of the modern infrastructure of the Oneida Nation.

"It didn't come without strife inside the tribe. There was internal bickering, too," Jerry said. "I thought what we did was great. But very few people know all the details of how we got here and what it's based on."

Nevertheless, bingo was an outstanding success. By early 1984, bingo games at the new IMAC facility were grossing between $120,000 and $150,000 a month, and cigarette sales brought in about $50,000 a month, according to the tribal treasurer. Bingo and tobacco income were a major source of the tribe's share of financing a proposed $10 million, two-hundred-room hotel and conference center next to the bingo center and across from Austin Straubel Airport. The Rodeway Inn, later renamed the Radisson Hotel and Conference Center, opened in June 1986 and remains owned and operated by a tribal enterprise, the Oneida Airport Hotel Corporation.

How big was bingo becoming? Each month Oneida Bingo was drawing thirty-seven thousand players. The biggest problem was trying to accommodate all who wanted to play. During an interview with a *Milwaukee Sentinel* business reporter in January 1984, Sandy Ninham was interrupted several times by phone calls. She had to turn down a couple of busloads of players who wanted admission for a Saturday evening.

"We had to go to advance sales for Saturday because people were driving in from 200 or more miles and had to be turned away," she told the reporter.[5]

In early 1985, the Oneida invited other tribes to see their high-stakes bingo operation at an open seminar. Among the tribes attending was the Mashantucket Pequot Indian Tribe of Ledyard, Connecticut. The Pequot tribe was planning to open a bingo hall on land restored in a 1983 federal land claims settlement and was suing the state for the right to offer bingo without state interference. The Pequot bingo hall would be managed by the Penobscot Indians of Maine for two years until the Pequots could run it on their own, Pequot tribal chairman Skip Hayward told the media.

The Oneida model was significant enough that the New London, Connecticut, newspaper *The Day* sent a reporter to visit the Wisconsin bingo operation in the spring of 1985.

"We put Oneida on the map with bingo," manager Sandy Ninham told *The Day* reporter. "It's a career for me, and it's a business for the tribe," she said.

Sandy's job now gave her the means to open her own checking account and buy things on her own. It gave her a measure of independence.

"I think she changed the perspective of a woman's role in her own family," her daughter Patty said. "Her mom was a stay-at-home mother of a Catholic family. While the boys went to work, the girls were expected to stay home with the kids." Patty said her mom's career changed those expectations and offered new dreams for future generations of girls like her. Many Oneida women worked outside the home, but few of them ran businesses.

While Sandy's career and the tribal business were on solid ground, her marriage was unraveling. In 1985, she and her husband, Lee, divorced after nearly twenty-four years of marriage. That spring, coincidentally, marked ten years since she and Alma Webster had made the unsuccessful bingo supply trip to Oshkosh when Sandy was pregnant with her fifth child, Matthew.

Bingo as a tribal enterprise had been born soon after Sandy's last son. The bingo operation, which started as a way to buy basketballs for tribal kids and keep the lights on at the Site I civic center, had grown up at the same time as her young family. Matthew was now ten and collected Star Wars action figures. Steve and Pamela had finished high school and were working part-time jobs. Tim attended Haskell Indian Junior College in Lawrence, Kansas, and later joined the navy. Patty was in college at Oshkosh and came home weekends to work bingo.

Sandy had managed to give her kids a strong and solid upbringing, but she had been unable to save her marriage. Lee moved out of the house he had built on Florist Drive. Sandy remained at the home along with Matthew. Several of her children returned to live at home with her for a time over the next few years.

"The kids rallied and came home to help take care of Matthew. I relied on Pamela a lot," Sandy said.

The split caused some friends and family to distance themselves from Sandy. She felt people avoided her as though divorce might be contagious. At times, Sandy felt alone and close to a breakdown.

"I remember I took a two- or three-week break from bingo," she said.

After the break, Sandy came back to work and threw herself into her job as bingo manager. Work provided some stability and assurance through times of personal upheaval. She also felt protective of bingo.

"I felt like it wouldn't go right without me there. It was my baby," she told me.

By early 1986, bingo games at the Irene Moore Activity Center provided work for 150 people. Construction of the two-hundred-room hotel employed another 160 people in Oneida. Bingo revenue and tobacco sales financed 88 percent of tribal programs.

"These kinds of economic self-sufficiency efforts and reinvestment are to be applauded," Democratic Governor Anthony Earl said during a 1986 tour of the Oneida tribe's bingo center and hotel project. While at the bingo hall, the governor took over the microphone during one session and called twenty-five numbers until a $160 winner was determined.[6]

"He's a pretty good caller," Sandy was quoted as telling the seven hundred players. "If he had just a little bit of Indian in him, we'd hire him."

In May of the following year, Wisconsin Republican governor Tommy Thompson visited the IMAC and sat down to play bingo with tribal officials. Thompson toured Oneida Tribal Enterprises, including the tribe's tobacco business, bingo hall, and the new $10 million Rodeway Inn.

Bingo players came to Oneida from Milwaukee, Madison, Michigan's Upper Peninsula, and the Fox River valley. Sandy gave credit for the success to the bingo staff, who she said were always friendly and ready to help customers. About 75 percent of all players were repeat customers or regulars "and I believe that is due as much to our friendliness as our big prizes," Sandy said.[7] The Oneida tribe had recently raised its bingo jackpot to $50,000.

One regular bingo player was Linda Lodel, who had been coming to Oneida Bingo since it was held at the civic center. Back then, she was in her twenties and usually came with girlfriends from Sheboygan.

Over the years, Linda got her brother involved and the pair would win fifty or a hundred dollars, she told me. She often played bingo with her grandma, Anna Groeschel. One time in about 1985, Anna fainted during a bingo game at Oneida. An ambulance was called to assist the eighty-five-year-old grandmother.

"In the ambulance, she came to and said, 'Aren't we staying for another session?'" Linda recalled. "That woman, she liked her bingo."

On April 17, 1987, a Friday night, Linda drove from her home thirty-six miles away in Chilton with a friend to play bingo at Oneida. Linda, thirty-three years old, married, and the mother of two, had cut back on her gambling because her full-time job at a Sheboygan plastics company was reduced to part-time. On that Friday, she was playing the "Do It Yourself" progressive bingo, in which players select seven numbers. If all seven are called before the sixteenth number is announced, the player wins the fifty-thousand-dollar grand prize.

For years, Linda played "Do It Yourself" progressive bingo. The numbers always were tied to family milestones, including the ages of herself, her husband, her thirteen-year-old son, and her ten-year-old daughter. When they called her seventh number on the twelfth ball racked, Linda was too excited to call bingo and just jumped up and down and yelled "I did it, I did it!" she later told a news reporter. She had won fifty thousand dollars, the biggest prize possible at the time, and was the first to win the "Do It Yourself" game. Her veteran status as a bingo player now confirmed, Linda was a true bingo queen.

"I felt like I was in a different world," she was quoted as saying. "It's something you dream about but never think will happen."

After taxes, she split the pot with her mother, June Groeschel of rural Chilton, because her mom paid half of her gambling expenses. She used the money to buy gifts for the kids, a trip with her husband to Las Vegas, and a family trip to Disney World.[8]

Linda said she called her husband, Henry, to tell him the news. "He didn't believe it. He kept saying, 'You're kidding, right?'"

Linda received a standing ovation from the crowd.

Louise King, night session supervisor at Oneida Bingo, came running out of the office with other workers when she heard someone had won the fifty-thousand-dollar jackpot.

"I've been telling people one of these days, it will go. We couldn't believe it," Louise told the *Green Bay Press-Gazette* the following week. The prize had been at fifty thousand dollars for several months.

Louise had grown up around bingo, too. In her early twenties, she worked as assistant building manager of the civic center in 1977 and as a bingo cashier and floorworker in 1978, earning ten or twenty dollars a session. She left in 1979, moved to Milwaukee, attended technical school, and was a stay-at-home mom to a son. She came back to Oneida and rejoined Oneida Bingo in October 1985 as a relief supervisor. She's been there ever since.

I interviewed Louise at a lunch in De Pere with Sandy and Alma. Louise recalled how in 1986, the bingo managers needed someone to be interviewed on TV and talk about an upcoming three-hundred-dollar bingo bash special. Alma wouldn't do it. She locked herself in her office; she preferred to run things behind the scenes.

"They pushed me out there," Louise said. "Sandy told me, 'You've got to do this. You're going to run this place someday.'"

When I interviewed her in 2010, Louise (King) Cornelius was gaming general manager for the Oneida Bingo/Casino. She was indeed running the place.

"My whole adult life has been in gaming, except for five years in Milwaukee," she said. Of her role in the development of Oneida gaming, she said, "I'm proud to be a part of it."

She said her biggest regret was missing any of her kids' sports or school events because of work.

With bingo growing in the 1980s, many tribal members saw an increased need for law enforcement services to better protect residents and visitors.

Historian L. Gordon McLester III said Oneida tribal law enforcement would have developed on its own sooner or later, but it would have been later without bingo.

"As bingo grew, so did the Oneida Police Department," Gordon told me. A tribal police force represented a significant step forward in tribal self-government.

Opportunities for crime grew along with bingo profits. One summer night in 1979, someone broke into an office in the civic center and made off with a weekend's worth of bingo money from a safe. The bingo managers were admonished about the need to lock doors. The Bingo Committee offered a five-hundred-dollar reward for information. Managers also looked into adding an alarm detection system and hiring more security guards.[9]

Vern Doxtator later helped lead bingo security improvements. Vern's mother, Audrey Doxtator, was administrator of the Oneida Health Center and was an early Bingo Committee member. Vern started working Oneida Bingo as a teen in 1978 selling cards at the civic center on weekends. His sisters, Debbie and Patty, worked as bingo callers. Back then, off-duty police officers Jim Danforth, Bill Sauer, Ted Hawk, Greg Powless, and Gary Ness worked part-time security for bingo. More security staff was needed after bingo moved to the IMAC.

The sheriff's departments in Brown and Outagamie Counties employed deputies on staff who were Oneida tribal members, but the local agencies were unable to provide the level of services tribal members requested for community law enforcement.[10] In 1985, Oneida leaders asked Jim Danforth, a tribal member and Outagamie County sheriff's deputy, to help create a tribal police force. The Oneida Public Safety Department, with Danforth as police chief, was established November 12, 1985. The goal was that the Oneida Nation would provide its own police, fire, and rescue services on the reservation. Thirteen officers, all of them enrolled Oneida members, completed law enforcement training at area technical schools. The first seven police officers hired had been bingo security personnel, Danforth told the *Kalihwisaks*.[11]

After 1985, bingo security was placed under the direction of the OPD. About 90 percent of bingo security staff eventually transferred into OPD positions. Vern Doxtator was later hired as head of security for Oneida Bingo. Officers were recruited and trained in defense and arrest tactics and as first responders for medical emergencies. They also handled traffic duties.

Security presence should be low-key but visible, Vern Doxtator said. "You open doors for people, say hello to them, let them know you're watching. That won't stop people from robbing you, but those are deterrents that can make your place look less appealing to them," he said.

Despite new security measures, scandals surfaced with reports that employees were skimming bingo and pull-tab profits. In 1988, several workers in the pull-tab section were disciplined for alleged theft of money. Tribal managers learned from the mistakes and made improvements in self-regulation. The new Oneida Police Department, meanwhile, met with some resistance from local law agencies whose boundaries overlapped the reservation's. The sheriff's departments in Brown and Outagamie Counties at first did not recognize the Oneida department as a law enforcement agency with arrest powers, and in 1987 Brown County Sheriff Leon Pieschek warned that Oneida police officers who responded to calls on the reservation could be arrested for interfering with his deputies.

Public Law 280 gave jurisdiction on criminal matters in Indian country to the state. Wisconsin's laws were enforced by county sheriffs, the departments said. But a suit by the two counties in federal court in 1987 determined the tribe had concurrent jurisdiction along with the counties on land within reservation boundaries. After that ruling, the Ashwaubenon Public

Safety Department agreed to provide dispatch services to Oneida. Brown County Sheriff Pieschek reversed his stand and entered a verbal agreement with Oneida in 1988 for dual dispatch. That meant a county officer and a tribal officer would be dispatched at the same time to respond to calls within the reservation.

But the issue wasn't over. Pieschek's move drew opposition from the Brown County Public Safety Committee and County Board chairman Guy Zima. In a *Green Bay News-Chronicle* story from December 29, 1988, Zima said he objected to the sheriff's agreement because he believed it was a step toward Oneida deputizing its own officers and could further legitimize Oneida as a government. Zima said the issue was not one of race but of jurisdiction, according to the newspaper. The county was considering filing a lawsuit to define tribal jurisdiction. The next month, the Brown County Board voted 23–19 to request Pieschek cancel the Oneida dual dispatch agreement. Pieschek refused.

"I took a lot of heat for that," Pieschek told me years later. "I was criticized by the County Board and Public Safety Committee."

Pieschek told the board he couldn't be concerned with a possible lawsuit. The tribe would pay the county nineteen thousand dollars a year under the contract to dispatch tribal officers from the county's communication center. "They have authority to establish a public safety department. . . . I have not given them any deputization or arrest authority," Pieschek said in a January 28, 1989, *News-Chronicle* story.

Outagamie County Sheriff Brad Gehring, meanwhile, agreed to a plan to dispatch Oneida officers in that county's part of the reservation. In most of the Outagamie cases the Oneida officers were dispatched alone, depending on the seriousness of the call. Eventually, Oneida officers were accepted as deputies with full arrest powers. By 1993, all Oneida police officers were cross-deputized as either Brown or Outagamie sheriff's deputies, depending on which county they lived in. Cross-deputization meant officers were authorized to enforce both tribal and state laws.

Cross-deputization and the dispatch agreement "really gave us the tools to enforce laws on the reservation," Danforth said. The Oneida Police Department now enjoys a positive relationship with all surrounding communities. Danforth said a significant moment for him was sitting down at a meeting next to the two county sheriffs and the police chief of Green Bay and being able to "have an equal say into things."[12]

Pieschek recalled having a good working relationship with Danforth. Pieschek served as Brown County sheriff from 1983 to 1993 and had been a patrol officer for Brown County for nearly twenty years before that. He started as a patrolman in 1964 in Oneida. In 1977, he bought an eleven-acre farmstead within the reservation boundaries along Duck Creek at Overland Road.

"There was never much trouble, some calls to the White Eagle bar or a dance hall. You could usually talk things out," he told me. After retiring as sheriff, Leon operated Pieschek Protective Services. He continued to live on Overland Road until 2010 when he and his wife, Mary, moved and sold the property to the Oneida Nation.

Leon Pieschek said he witnessed the tribe's growth and development during that time. "It's like day and night," he said. "Back then there was no prosperity, no jobs. The Oneidas grew from that and became organized, became good neighbors. I supported them. I deputized their officers into the sheriff's department. We had to make sure they were qualified and that they met the same criteria as our officers. If they didn't, they couldn't make arrests. Now their officers can testify in county courts."

In 1984, Pieschek was cutting wood on his property adjoining Duck Creek when he injured himself with a chainsaw. The first county deputy to respond on the scene was an Oneida officer, he told me.

Bingo in Indian country was at its peak in 1987, but something even bigger was coming. That year, voters in Wisconsin approved a statewide referendum to create a state lottery, which would later open the door to Class III Indian casinos in the state.

The Cabazon and Morongo bingo lawsuit that started in California in 1980 prevailed in lower courts. The state of California continued to appeal, and the Supreme Court accepted the case in 1986.

"When all of this began in 1980, I don't think any of us realized at the time that this was something we might have to take all the way to the

Supreme Court," said Glenn Feldman, attorney for Cabazon. "There had already been two earlier cases, one out of Florida involving the Seminoles and one out of Wisconsin involving the Oneidas, in which the question of tribal rights to operate gaming had been litigated. Both those cases were bingo operations on the reservation, and the tribes had won those cases. So there was some precedent for our position in the lower courts, but for a variety of reasons this became the case that went all the way to the Supreme Court, although I don't think any of us understood or anticipated that was going to happen. Maybe one of the answers is that California was a tougher opponent than Florida or Wisconsin had been."[13]

The Cabazon litigation was closely watched by tribes and states alike. Nearly half the country, twenty-one states, supported California's position,[14] but in a 6–3 opinion in 1987, the Supreme Court ruled the Cabazon and Morongo bingo halls could operate outside state law. States had no jurisdiction over Class II bingo halls and lacked authority over most Class III casino gaming as well, the high court ruled. Any gaming regulation would have to come from the US Congress, not the states.

"When Cabazon was handed down, I was elated. Surprised. Oh, my God. I was in shock. Everyone was in shock, just struck by lightning. Conversely, the opposition was beyond angry," Franklin Ducheneaux, a member of the Cheyenne River Sioux Tribe of South Dakota and counsel to the House Interior Committee, was quoted as saying.[15]

In response to the Cabazon decision, Congress passed the Indian Gaming Regulatory Act (IGRA) in 1988, which gave leverage to states in negotiating casinos on Indian land. IGRA said Class I traditional games were under sole tribal jurisdiction. Class II gaming, such as bingo, is regulated by tribes with oversight by the National Indian Gaming Commission. Class III gaming, such as slot machines, blackjack, and roulette, is subject to IGRA requirements, including state-tribal compacts, which states are required to negotiate in good faith.

Within a month of IGRA's passage, Oneida chairman Purcell Powless contacted Wisconsin's governor about getting a Class III gaming compact in Oneida. It would take nearly three years. Purcell retired in 1990; the following year the Oneida and the state entered a compact that would allow a casino. The compact was negotiated by the new tribal chairman, Rick Hill, and vice chairperson Debbie (Skenandore) Doxtator, who were elected in

1990. The Oneida Casino, adjoining the Radisson Hotel across from the airport, opened in 1993.

After Rick Hill became NIGA chairman in 1993, Debbie was elected to two terms as Oneida tribal chairperson, serving from 1993 to 1999. She was the tribe's second woman chair, following in the footsteps of her great-aunt, Irene Moore.

Casino gaming continued the economic development begun under bingo. In just twenty years, the Oneida Nation of Wisconsin transformed from having one of the highest unemployment rates in the state to becoming the largest employer in Brown County. After expanding into casino gambling, the tribe was employing 3,350 people by 1997, including 1,200 non-Indians and 300 non-Oneida Indians. Two-fifths of the workforce was in gaming. The rest, about 1,900 people, worked in other tribal programs and enterprises, according to a 1997 Wisconsin Policy Research Institute Report titled "Impact of Indian Casino Gambling on Metropolitan Green Bay," by Daniel Alesch. Casino employment was largely credited for cutting the poverty rate among the Wisconsin Oneida from 50 percent to 5 percent between 1990 and 2000.[16]

In 2011, Indian gaming generated $27.2 billion in revenue among 237 gaming tribes, the National Indian Gaming Commission reported. The upper Midwest region is known for having modest, though the most numerous, Indian casino operations nationwide. All eleven federally recognized tribes in Wisconsin have gaming operations.

The Oneida economic model, while not perfect, is a good example of modern tribalism, said James M. Murray, professor emeritus of economics at the University of Wisconsin–Green Bay. Murray, who worked as an economic development consultant to the Oneida, said the Oneida model combines elements of capitalism and utopian socialism. According to Murray, the late Vine Deloria Jr. and Ernest Stevens Sr. wrote and thought about tribalism not as simply a traditional organization of past Indian communities, but as a model for a better future for all societies.[17]

The Oneida worked hard to build their reputation as a viable and relevant contributor to the Wisconsin economy and community. In the late 1990s the Green Bay Packers—the only community-owned team in the NFL— floated a $295 million plan to renovate Lambeau Field. The team said the update was needed to remain financially competitive in the NFL. Brown County voters approved a 0.5 percent county sales tax to finance the plan in September 2000. As a result of a second referendum two months later, the team found itself under pressure to sell naming rights to the stadium as a way to minimize the tax burden on residents. But many fans wanted to keep the stadium named for the team's cofounder, Curly Lambeau. The team instead sold naming rights to gate entrances. The Oneida Nation sponsored one of the first five gates at Lambeau Field. The Oneida Nation entrance facing Oneida Street was a visible sign that the tribe had a seat at the table as a business partner and good neighbor in the community.

Ernest Stevens Jr., who as a rebellious teenager opposed bingo in the civic center, eventually returned to Oneida. The former gaming opponent would become its biggest advocate, serving for years as chief spokesman for all gaming tribes as chairman of the National Indian Gaming Association.

"Indian gaming offers hope for the future," Ernie said. While gaming is not a cure-all for tribes, it has helped create jobs; fund the building of housing, nursing homes, and health centers; and provide educational scholarships, he said. The Oneida also used gaming profits to help build a police station, child-care centers, farms, and a string of convenience stores, and to buy a golf course and a bank.

After Ernie grew to be an adult and father and had moved back to Oneida in the late 1980s, he finally got to know his own father better. Both men served on Oneida boards, councils, and commissions in the 1990s and often met for breakfast at the tribal-owned Radisson Hotel. Their favorite spot was Table 21, a prominent round table at the front of the restaurant.

"We talk, you buy," Ernest Sr. would tell Ernie when they sat down to a meal. When Ernie ran for the National Congress of American Indians in 1995, his father told him not to become one of those "conference Indians" who attend mainly for the meals and entertainment. "He told me, 'You have to show up, work, and help.' That's something I never forgot," Ernie said. He has served as chairman of the National Indian Gaming Association since 2001. He still sees his dad almost daily, although Ernest Sr. suffered a stroke several years ago and can't get around much. I usually met Ernie for interviews at Table 21, the spot where he used to meet his dad.

"It's kind of ironic. Even though my father was absent, he played a very significant role in my life," Ernie told me. "They say I look like my father. My mom told me I was going to be just like my dad when I grew up. But I'm also a lot like my mother. I'm Marjie Jr. right here," he said, thumping a fist to his heart. "My mother was always an activist. She took strong positions, led protests, and helped start the Indian Community School in Milwaukee. She said I need to conduct myself as a statesman and always be a gentleman.

"I'm a strong-willed person," Ernie added. "I may go too far. But we're still in that matrilineal world. It's my wife, Cheryl, who empowers me, allows me to be who I am. And if I overassert my authority, my wife will call me on it. I am who I am because I was raised by very powerful Oneida women.

"These ladies, the bingo queens, kept moving the message forward to provide for our community," Ernie said. "In poor families, fathers often had to leave home to find work," he noted. "It may have looked like women were doing all the work, but their husbands were out in the field, or the factory, or in Purcy's case on the high steel. I don't think there's any domineering other than the natural part of Oneida women playing an equal role. I think that's what women did to make a better place. They didn't have time to wait for husbands to get home. In Oneida, women had a natural leadership responsibility. They had to make something happen."

Ernie, the former boxer, now uses his fists metaphorically to fight for Indian unity, sovereignty, and sobriety. Ernie has been alcohol- and drug-free since 1988 and his leadership also is known for setting an example to others to break the chains of addiction.

Sandy Ninham eventually remarried, to construction project manager Mike Brehmer, and moved to Florida. Her ex-husband, Lee, also remarried. He and his second wife, Rebecca, adopted and raised two children, Rachel and Eli. Lee left the paper mills in 1995 and took a job with the Oneida tribe hearing employee grievances. That body evolved into the current Oneida Tribal Judicial System.

Lee Ninham became a tribal judge in 1999. As a young father, he had given up his dream of college and went to work in the mills after high school. In 2000, he finally got a college diploma. He earned a management-communications degree from Concordia College. At age seventy, Lee started a consulting business focusing on peacemaking. Gaming revenue paid for his training as a judge and allowed him to travel to other reservations during his eight-year tenure as head of the Wisconsin Tribal Judges Association.

But the Oneida also have endured conflicts and setbacks. Relations with neighboring communities have been strained. The Oneida lost a federal court case in 1992 to operate TV Bingo Oneida because sales of cards occurred outside the reservation. Several nongaming tribal ventures or collaborations lost money and failed. Local municipalities continue to object to the tribe placing reacquired parcels into federal trust because it takes land off the public tax rolls. After downturns in the national economy in 2001 and 2008, the Oneida Nation dropped to the fifth-largest employer in Brown County.[18]

Gaming has had negative impacts on the state, too. The Wisconsin Council on Problem Gambling estimated that problem or compulsive gamblers make up between 5 and 7 percent of Wisconsin's population, or about 333,000 people. The Green Bay–based council is funded by a state public awareness grant plus donations from Wisconsin's Indian tribes to provide help to problem gamblers. The council's helpline (1-800-GAMBLE-5) fielded more than 14,000 calls in 2010. About 65 percent of compulsive gamblers commit crimes to finance their gambling, said Rose Gruber, executive director of the council. The Oneida Bingo & Casino provides brochures and online links (www.wi-problemgamblers.org).

Yet gaming jobs and a strong tribal infrastructure helped draw many Oneida back to the reservation to invest their lives in the community. The Oneida diaspora was being reversed. Oneidas were returning to the rez. The Oneida Nation of Wisconsin now has 16,500 members, with about half that number living on or near the reservation. Gaming helped keep the lights burning on the reservation.

"I feel really good about our efforts. It helped change the direction for the tribe. Young people have more opportunities," Sandy said.

One example of the opportunities that gaming offered is Raeann Skenandore, an Oneida who grew up in Milwaukee. She was a mom to two small kids by her early twenties, and in the 1980s she wanted to move back to Oneida. She interviewed for a job at bingo at the IMAC. During the interview she was asked why she wanted to work bingo.

"I told them I needed to work to feed my family," Raeann said. The job paid a little better than minimum wage. She quickly earned more as a bingo caller.

"The experience told me I wanted more," she said. She moved on to an administrative job in the tribal law office and later became retail supervisor in Oneida's Tsyunhehkwa health store.

"Gaming helped bring back a lot of people," Alma Webster said.

Sandy's oldest daughter, Patty, is proud of her mom's contributions to the Oneida community. She feels it's the responsibility of future generations to build on those foundations.

"I think Oneida Bingo helped secure the community in its place and keep the people together," Patty said. "It was a source of jobs. It gave the people of the tribe a reason to stay put on Duck Creek and grow their families here—because they easily could have continued the trend to migrate to urban areas if there was no work. I think Oneida would look totally different without it. People who are grandparents now are celebrating thirty years of employment with the tribe. I think that's incredible."

The physical place where the Oneida grow up is very important, Patty added. "Families are growing up in the same place, side by side, and have a collective, shared experience, something in common. It's about kinships. I think that's the glue that defines how it is to be Oneida. We're like salmon. You have to come back to the same place to start a family. So you need a good habitat. That's how we define our sustainability; it's building a strong place. When Oneidas do leave and move someplace else for a while, they know there's always a place to come home to."

Bingo's heyday lasted a little over a decade; the casino's has lasted two decades and more.

"So what's the next new idea that will emerge that will bring everyone together again and give us purpose for continuing to stay here? What's the next bingo? I'm keeping my eye open for that," Patty said.

Oneida Bingo grew from a seed planted by a group of women who were trying to pay the light bill at the tribe's civic center. It did that and much more.

Notes

1. After working as a comedy writer in Los Angeles for decades, Charlie Hill moved back to Oneida in 2010. I remember this joke from his

standup routines in the late 1980s and early 1990s. When I asked him if I could use the joke in my book, Charlie said he couldn't take all the credit. He said he based his joke on an observation Vine Deloria Jr. had made. Deloria's book, *Red Earth, White Lies*, starts with a chapter called "Behind the Buckskin Curtain." "When Indian bingo games are humming in almost every nook and cranny of our land, stealing the most sacred ritual of the Roman Catholic Church and gathering the white man's coin as quickly as it can reasonably be retrieved, progress is being made," Deloria wrote. Vine Deloria Jr., *Red Earth, White Lies* (Golden, CO: Fulcrum, 1997).

2. *Oneida Tribe v. Wisconsin*, 518 F. Supp. 712 (W.D. Wis. 1981).

3 "Court OKs Oneidas' Bingo," *Green Bay Press-Gazette*, June 17, 1982.

4. Suzette Brewer, ed., *Sovereign: An Oral History of Indian Gaming in America* (Albuquerque, NM: Ipanema Literatures, 2009).

5. Thomas Murphy, "Bingo Spurs Hotel Project of Oneida Indians," *Milwaukee Sentinel*, January 18, 1984.

6. "Earl Lauds Oneidas' Projects," *Green Bay Press-Gazette*, January 11, 1986.

7. *Milwaukee Sentinel*, January 18, 1984.

8. "Woman Wins $50,000 Bingo Prize," *Milwaukee Journal*, April 21, 1987.

9. Bingo Committee meeting minutes, August 10, 1979, Audrey Doxtator, secretary.

10. Artley Skenandore Sr. was the first enrolled Oneida to be elected Brown County sheriff. He served as sheriff from 1957 to 1960.

11. "Hail, and Farewell, to the Chief," *Kalihwisaks*, February 20, 2003.

12. Ibid.

13. Brewer, *Sovereign*.

14. Charles Wilkinson, *Blood Struggle: The Rise of Modern Indian Nations* (New York: W.W. Norton & Co., 2005).

15. Brewer, *Sovereign*.

16. Chuck Nowlen, "Casinos Bring Benefits," *Capital Times*, Madison, Wisconsin, January 20, 2004.

17. Jim Murray, *A Wasicu (White Man) in Indian Country* (Xlibris, 2012).

18. "Tribes of Wisconsin," Wisconsin Department of Administration, Division of Intergovernmental Relations, July 2011.

Epilogue

Fall 2010

IN HIS last days, Purcell Powless regularly saw people for a few hours a day. Jerry L. Hill stopped to visit; Francis Skenandore came by several times. Milton Rosenberg came from Madison to Purcell's funeral in November.

Near the end, Purcell told his family, "'I'm ready to go. I've lived a good life. I have no regrets,'" his daughter Bobbi Webster recalled. "He made us accept it, the way he went."

Purcell sat up in his recliner until the very end of his life. Cleo and Wayne Cornelius stopped to visit him two weeks before he passed and brought him a gift bag, Bobbi said. Among the items was a deck of cards and a verse about how each card represented some facet of the Bible. That gift made Bobbi remember a song about a deck of cards that a soldier used as a Bible. "It was a country-western song and I don't remember who sang it, but it was old. Dad's eyes were closed but he was listening and without missing a beat he said it was Tex Ritter. That moment reminded me what a wise and wonderful man Dad was and how his mind was sharp and his memory never failed him, or me. When I didn't know someone in the community, I always called him up and said, 'Dad, who were they related to?' He always knew."

Sandy told me that even though more Oneida are moving back to the reservation, some of them have less connection to the community; they are strangers to one another. But that's not how it used to be.

According to Bobbi, in the old days people like her dad called on neighbors to help build their houses and work on projects they couldn't afford to hire out or do alone.

"They'd come on a Saturday and work and drink and eat. He bought the lumber, and my mom cooked all the food. Then my dad would be gone the next weekend helping someone else on their house," she said. "These people took care of each other. That ethic, that family value, we're losing it." There's a perception now that the tribe will care for you. It's created a lack of appreciation, she said.

"Now people say, 'I don't have to help my neighbor. The tribe's going to build me a bathroom. I don't have to help my brother or sister. The tribe will provide for me.' Dad would never ask the tribe for anything," she said.

Purcell was not one for fancy suits or cars. He got new siding on his house and said he enjoyed having a snowblower in the winter. "The only thing Purcell wanted from the tribe was having the hotel lounge named after him," Ada Deer told me. Today you can see signs in the Radisson announcing "Purcell's Lounge" and "Purcy's Porch."

An ongoing debate in Oneida is whether gaming revenue should continue to be invested in community infrastructure and jobs or distributed in annual per capita payments to individual tribal members as a kind of corporate dividend. Oneida per capita payments have ranged between $800 and $1,200 a year.

In other words, should gaming revenue be used to benefit the community or the individual? Sandy said there's a feeling today that people are in it more for themselves and are less connected to the Oneida community.

"Some people don't know how to make their success our success," Sandy said.

As Purcell Powless passed the torch to younger leaders, the bingo queens, too, made way for a new generation.

Alma took over as bingo manager when Sandy transferred to a new tribal position in marketing. Alma oversaw the installation of slot machines in the IMAC as the tribe expanded into casino gaming. Sandy was elected to the Business Committee in 1993 and served six years on the council. She later served on the Oneida Gaming Commission.

Sandy and Alma both retired from positions in tribal leadership at the end of 2001. Alma stays quietly busy in the community and still plays bingo. But she's firm about not wanting credit for it. "I told my husband that when I go, I don't want any mention of it," she told me.

Women like Alma run silent and deep, Bobbi Webster said. "They're humble and didn't ask for recognition. They didn't promote themselves and say, 'I was there, I did that.' There was no glory seeking, no gimme per capita. They didn't have dollar signs in their eyes; they had vision," she said.

Sandy said it's important not to lose sight of why bingo started in the first place: to build a community where people want to grow together.

Adapting to new environments, mixing old approaches with new are longstanding Indian responses to challenges. Women pursue careers long held by men. Mothers teach culinary skills to sons. High-steel workers hand their tool belts to daughters.

Today, the Oneida are harvesting crops in a blend of traditional ways and modern lifestyles. In the old days, Haudenosaunee matrons supervised the cornfields. Now a largely male staff led by Jeff Metoxen runs the Tsyunhehkwa organic farm. Staff agriculturist Ted Skenandore is experimenting with aquaponics, in which filtered water is used to raise fish and fertilize crops in a symbiotic system. At an Oneida food sovereignty conference, tribes such as the Leech Lake Band of Ojibwe and the Menominee Nation shared stories on restoring wild rice beds. The Oneida shared tips on growing traditional white corn. One of the people attending was John Kane, a native activist from New York. He told me he believes the economic future for indigenous people lies in agriculture. In other words, corn could be the new bingo.

The Oneida are reviving old ways to connect people. Each fall, the public is invited to help harvest the Oneida corn crop in a community event. Non-Indians in the community, many from local churches or schools, help Indians pick corn. People sit on folding chairs in a circle under a big tent and chat while they work. They peel back the dry cornhusks, smooth them into a tail, and stack the ears in piles. The farm's staff members braid the tails into long strands that are hung from barn rafters to dry. Workers at the cannery process the corn kernels into fresh food. Corn products and other food are available for sale daily at two Oneida stores. "I tell people this is our Oneida fast food: cornbread, fresh hull corn, and berry corn mush," said Oneida Cannery supervisor Vickie Cornelius. "We started selling it every day because it is our traditional food that I believe should be eaten every week, not only on holidays."

After the corn is put away in the fall to dry, people in Oneida prepare for a long, cold winter. Traditionally, winter was a time for telling stories around a fire. Elders pass on lessons to younger generations in the form of stories. Bingo players still pack the Irene Moore Activity Center in Oneida, although bingo is no longer the top game in town. It's been eclipsed by Class III games like blackjack, slot machines, and card games at the Oneida Casino next door to the hotel.

The sound of bouncing basketballs—not bingo calls—echoes today through the old gymnasium in the Oneida civic center in Site I.

I met with Sandy and Alma at the civic center one winter afternoon for an interview. Being interviewed was still painful for Alma.

"I almost didn't come. I told my husband before I came here that I don't want to do this," she said. But she showed up nonetheless.

"She doesn't want to do this public kind of stuff," Sandy said. "I remember she locked herself in her office when the *Press-Gazette* came out to do a story."

"Oh, I hated it," Alma said. "After you were gone I'd have to take over every now and then on the mic." She found that her words would just disappear. "I'd get up there and, poof, it's gone."

"You always did good, so confident and clear with your message," Sandy told her. "I wouldn't have done all this stuff if not for her," Sandy said to me.

"And I wouldn't have done it if not for her," Alma said, gesturing to Sandy. "She's the one who got the gab out there."

"But I wouldn't gab if I didn't have the confident person behind me to say, 'This is what we're doing,'" Sandy replied.

"She always wants the last word," Alma said.

Index

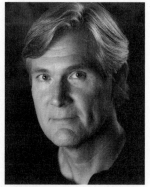

Dennis King/Dkingofimagez.com

MIKE HOEFT is an award-winning writer who retired after twenty-three years as reporter and copy editor at the *Green Bay Press-Gazette* covering courts, county government, and public safety. He is also the son-in-law of bingo manager Sandra Ninham.